To Russel

Ho
Up a

TOBY YOUNG

PENGUIN BOOKS

PENGUIN BOOKS

Published by the Penguin Group
Penguin Books Ltd, 80 Strand, London WC2R 0RL, England
Penguin Group (USA) Inc., 375 Hudson Street, New York, New York 10014, USA
Penguin Group (Canada), 90 Eglinton Avenue East, Suite 700, Toronto, Ontario, Canada M4P 2Y3
(a division of Pearson Penguin Canada Inc.)
Penguin Ireland, 25 St Stephen's Green, Dublin 2, Ireland (a division of Penguin Books Ltd)
Penguin Group (Australia), 707 Collins Street, Melbourne, Victoria 3008, Australia
(a division of Pearson Australia Group Pty Ltd)
Penguin Books India Pvt Ltd, 11 Community Centre, Panchsheel Park, New Delhi – 110 017, India
Penguin Group (NZ), 67 Apollo Drive, Rosedale, Auckland 0632, New Zealand
(a division of Pearson New Zealand Ltd)
Penguin Books (South Africa) (Pty) Ltd, Block D, Rosebank Office Park,
181 Jan Smuts Avenue, Parktown North, Gauteng 2193, South Africa

Penguin Books Ltd, Registered Offices: 80 Strand, London WC2R 0RL, England

www.penguin.com

First published as an electronic edition in Penguin Books 2011
Published, with revisions, in Penguin Books 2012
001

Set in 11/13 pt Bembo Book MT Std
Typeset by Jouve (UK), Milton Keynes
Printed in England by Clays Ltd, St Ives plc

ISBN: 978–0–241–96533–7

www.greenpenguin.co.uk

PENGUIN BOOKS

HOW TO SET UP A FREE SCHOOL

Toby Young is the lead proposer, co-founder and Chair of Governors of the West London Free School, England's first free school to sign a Funding Agreement with the Secretary of State for Education. When he's not advising people how to set up free schools, he is an associate editor of the *Spectator* and a columnist for the *Sun*. He is the author of the international bestseller *How to Lose Friends and Alienate People* and co-produced the film of the same name starring Jeff Bridges, Simon Pegg and Kirsten Dunst. He lives in Acton with his wife and four children.

To Andrew Adonis and Michael Gove, without whom none of this would have been possible

Contents

Author's Note

I wrote the first edition of this book in the autumn of 2011, at which point twenty-four free schools had opened and a further sixty-five had been approved to open in 2012. For the new edition, I've updated it to reflect the fact that at least a dozen of that second batch have had to defer for a year and some are unlikely to open at all. I've also tried to find out what I can about the third wave of free schools that have been approved to open in 2013 and beyond. I've learnt a bit more about the set-up process since writing the first edition, having submitted a proposal to start a second free school – a primary this time, rather than a secondary. That school was among the 102 to be approved in the third batch.

This book is meant for small groups of volunteers, like the group I've been leading since 2009. It's not intended for corporate, multi-academy sponsors or for independent schools hoping to convert. Given how complex the set-up process has become, I'm worried that the policy will be hijacked by large, professional organisations and my reason for writing this book is to try to give parent groups a fighting chance. Don't just rely on this, though. You should also read the how-to material produced by the Department for Education and the New Schools Network, all of which is excellent and can be download from their websites. This book is intended to complement their advice, not be a substitute for it.

Introduction

You'll encounter many lows in the course of trying to set up a free school, but the lowest point for me was when Jonathan Fingerhut, a fifty-five-year-old marketing executive from Kentish Town, came to talk to our steering group. This was on 30 November 2009, and at that stage we didn't have a clue what we were doing. I'd written an article for the *Observer* three months earlier saying I wanted to start a 'comprehensive grammar' in Ealing and a group of local parents had volunteered to help. But after the initial burst of enthusiasm it had begun to dawn on us that setting up a state secondary school is a mammoth undertaking. There were initially fifteen people in the group, but by the time 30 November rolled around we were down to single figures. The whole project was in danger of fizzling out.

I thought a pep talk from Jonathan was just what the doctor ordered. He was an ordinary dad with no background in education, yet he had successfully led the efforts of a group of parents in north London to establish a liberal, Jewish comprehensive – or JCoSS, as it's now called. He'd faced down a multitude of opponents, including a group of ultra-conservative Orthodox Jews, and a brand-new school was now being built by the government on Castlewood Road in New Barnet. If anyone could revive my group's flagging spirits, it was him.

'Don't take this the wrong way,' he began, 'but before

you embark on this journey you have to ask yourselves whether this is really something you want to do. Because it took my group ten years to set up JCoSS. That's ten years of mind-numbing, back-breaking labour. Ten years of our lives we can never get back.'

As he paused to let his words sink in, I looked round at my colleagues. They were exchanging knowing looks, as if to say, 'What did I tell you?'

This was not going to plan.

'But, Jonathan,' I said. 'Presumably, if you knew you'd have a brand-new school at the end of it, a school embodying your vision and your ethos, you wouldn't have done anything any differently. It's all been worth it, right?'

He looked at me sceptically.

'Are you joking? My kids are too old to go to the school, I'm virtually bankrupt and it's seriously damaged my health. No, if I'd known then what I know now, I never would have gone down this road in the first place.'

Silence. Tumbleweeds.

'OK, right. Well, that's an *interesting* perspective. Would anyone like some more wine?'

In retrospect, I should have realized that any parent who's just been through the process of setting up a state school isn't going to be a great advocate for the cause and, in the course of writing this little book, I've had to guard against being too downbeat myself. It's a laborious, time-consuming process that will take over your life. Your family will suffer and friends will fall by the wayside, unable to grasp why your Friday nights are now spent sitting round your kitchen table discussing planning regulations. Whenever I bumped into other free-school proposers during this period we used to complain about how long it had been since we'd read a Sunday newspaper or gone to the cinema. We would joke about how bleary-eyed and exhausted we looked – 'free school-itis', we called it. The Big Society = Little Sleep.

One of the reasons it's so tough is that you're constantly having to deal with stony-faced bureaucrats who regard parents as meddling busybodies who have no place in public education. I remember telling the councillor in charge of education in Ealing that the attitude of a powerful official in his department had gone from 'aggressive to neutral'.

'If you've got him to neutral that's a tremendous achievement,' he said.

He was only half joking.

For ordinary civilians unversed in the jargon of the public sector, meeting civil servants for the first time is like encountering a strange new species. A week before Jonathan Fingerhut's 'pep talk' I'd had my first meeting at the DCSF – officially, the Department for Children, Schools and Families, but known in Whitehall as the Department for Chairs and Soft Furnishings. I came out with my head spinning. Apparently, my group was engaged in an effort to set up a 4FE (4-Form Entry) PPS (Parent Promoted School) and our fate turned on whether we could convince PfS (Partnerships for Schools) that the PPP (Pupil Place Planning) of Ealing Council's DCS (Director of Children's Services) had underestimated the expected increase in demand for secondary-school places in the borough over the next ten years. If we could, then BSF (Building Schools for the Future) might fund a 'new build'. Or perhaps the money would come from the SCS (Schools Capital Stream).

Back then, the process in place for the establishment of

new, state-funded schools was designed to be navigated by professional bureaucrats, not amateurs like me. There was simply no portal through which a group of unpaid volunteers could enter the process. Emerging from meetings at Ealing Town Hall, I often felt like a spaceman who'd spent the previous two hours trying to dock with a space station that had been designed to dock only with other space stations – and I was running out of oxygen.

Our group had decided our best bet was to try to set up a city academy – the new type of school established by the Learning and Skills Act 2000 – but there was no guarantee we'd be successful. It had taken eight years for Tony Blair's government to establish the first seventeen academies and by the end of Labour's third term only 209 had been created, most of them converters rather than new schools. No academy had ever been set up by a group of parents.

Back then, the official term for parents who wanted to start schools was 'parent promoters'. Apart from JCoSS – a voluntary aided (VA) school, rather than an academy – only one other state secondary school had been established by a group of 'parent promoters' under New Labour: the Elmgreen School in Lambeth, also a VA school. They'd managed it in four years, thanks to the unstinting support of Andrew Adonis, Tony Blair's 'academies tsar' in the DCSF. Unfortunately, Gordon Brown had moved him to the Department for Transport by the time we arrived on the scene and Ed Balls had been installed as the new Secretary of State.

Under Balls, the only funding route available to groups who wanted to set up new academies was BSF, an ambitious capital programme launched in 2003 with the aim of rebuilding or refurbishing all the secondary schools in England by 2020. In theory, that shouldn't have been a problem since Labour had set aside £55 billion to finance the programme, but applying for BSF funding was, in the words of a 2010 government report, 'complex, time-consuming, expensive and opaque'. According to the *Review of Education Capital*, it took a local authority, on average, 18–20 months to fill out all the paperwork and cost £1.7 million in terms of salaries, consultancy fees and so on. Even seasoned bureaucrats regarded the process as excessively bureaucratic. It was nigh-on impossible for a group of unpaid volunteers to navigate the process.

In order to qualify for BSF 'investment', the first thing you had to do was prove that there was a 'basic need' for additional school places in your borough – in other words, that there wasn't enough capacity in the borough's existing secondary schools to accommodate the anticipated growth in demand. In our case, that was relatively straightforward thanks to London's growing population. Ealing Council was scrabbling to find sufficient primary-school places and they'd soon be facing the same problem at secondary level.

More difficult was persuading the council to endorse our proposal for a new academy. One of the first things Ed Balls did on becoming Secretary of State in 2007 was to strengthen the oversight local authorities enjoyed over the creation of new academies. Indeed, academy sponsors couldn't even enter the set-up process without their local authority's blessing. That was a problem for us. In 2009, Ealing was Conservative-controlled but it made little difference. As with most councils, it's the officers who call the shots in Ealing, not the members. (If *Yes Minister* had been set in local government it would have been a documentary, not a sitcom.) We had no difficulty persuading these Town Hall Sir Humphreys of the basic need for a new secondary school in the area – they were perfectly aware of that. What we couldn't convince them of was that it should be set up and run by us. They thought they could do a better job themselves.

We were in the midst of a long and seemingly interminable negotiation when the general election was called for 6 May 2010. That was good news for us because the Conservatives, who looked set to romp home at that point, were proposing to make it easier for parents and other voluntary groups to set up academies – or 'free schools', as they were now being called. (There's really no difference between an academy and a free school – it's just a clever bit of re-branding so the Tories can take ownership of Tony Blair's most successful public service reform.) Indeed, one of the reasons we'd decided our best bet was to try to start an academy rather than go the JCoSS or Elmgreen route is because we were expecting the Conservatives to win the election and simplify the academy set-up process. We knew we'd be at the mercy of Ealing Council while Ed Balls was still in charge at the DCSF, but we hoped that one of the first actions of an incoming Tory Secretary of State would be to remove the local authority veto. I eagerly anticipated the day when I could stride into Ealing Town Hall and tell the army of officials to get stuffed.

You can imagine my disappointment, therefore, when the result of the election was a hung Parliament. In the five days that followed, I tracked the Conservative–Lib Dem talks obsessively, using all my journalistic and political contacts to try to discover exactly what role was being carved out for local authorities in the establishment of free schools. Would the veto remain in place, as many Lib Dem activists wanted? Or would Michael Gove have enough political clout to draw a 'red line' underneath the free-schools policy as set out in the Conservative manifesto? It wasn't until twenty-four hours after Gove's appointment as the Secretary of State for Education that we learned the veto had gone.

After the change of government, setting up a 'parent promoted' academy became a bit easier, but it was far from plain sailing. For one thing, there was the ferocious political opposition. Another low point was debating with the local NUT shop steward in front of Ealing Council's Education Scrutiny Panel. Just before I was due to appear I discovered he'd circulated a document to everyone on the panel falsely accusing me of sleeping with prostitutes.

As an out-of-the-closet Conservative, I was accustomed to the *Sturm und Drang* of party politics, but it was still a shock to find myself the subject of vicious personal attacks. In the *Guardian* I was caricatured as a 'Tory squire' who thought my precious children might be contaminated if they had to rub shoulders with the hoi polloi at the local comp. Apparently, I'd decided to set up a free school so Sasha, Ludo, Freddie and Charlie – such ghastly, middle-class names – could receive the equivalent of a private-school education at the taxpayers' expense.

In fact, the main reason I'd embarked on the project was because I wanted my children to be educated in the state sector, just as I had been. I didn't want them to be brought up in a bubble, surrounded by the sons and daughters of the plutocratic elite. But at the same time I also wanted them to receive an academically rigorous education where they'd be taught Latin and History and introduced to the best that had been thought and said. There were some state schools like that in west London, but they were either grammar schools or faith schools. What few comprehensives there were that offered a good old-fashioned liberal education were so over-subscribed you needed to live within a hundred yards of the school gates to stand a chance of getting in.

The pivotal moment for me was when my wife Caroline sat me down and said we'd have to move to the country. She'd found a really good comprehensive in Suffolk and worked out where we'd have to live in order to get our children in. She'd even made some inquiries with a local estate agent. At first, I grudgingly accepted this, but then I thought, *Hang on a minute. This is ridiculous. Why should we have to turn our lives upside down and move halfway across the country to get our children into a decent state school? If the state won't provide us with a good local school that all the children in the neighbourhood have access to, regardless of income, ability or faith, then we should bloody well start one ourselves.*

That may strike some people as arrogant – I prefer to think of it as stubborn – but I had a positive role model in the form of my late father, Michael Young. In addition to being a lifelong socialist and Labour Party panjandrum, he was a social entrepreneur who'd helped set up over sixty useful organizations including the Social Science Research Council, the Consumers' Association and *Which?* magazine. But his greatest claim to fame is that he'd come up with the idea for the Open University, now Europe's largest academic institution. If my father had managed to establish a university, how difficult could it be to start a secondary school?

In one sense, my motivation was selfish. I didn't want to move to Suffolk, I wanted a good local school that I could send my children to. But there was also something more complex going on. As mid-life had come upon me, I'd been gripped by the desire to do something good. A few years earlier I'd become a trustee of a blindness charity, but it wasn't enough. I wanted to put something back, to create an institution that would be of lasting benefit to my community. I wanted to do something that my father would have been proud of.

It was this, I think, that made the attacks from my father's beloved Labour Party so hard to take. Yes, making it easier for groups of volunteers to set up taxpayer-funded schools was a Conservative policy, but I naively thought free schools would be embraced by Labour as well. After all, the idea that people should take more responsibility for their lives, should become the authors of their own destinies, was common to both parties. A group of parents coming together and giving up their time to start a school that would be accessible to all children in the local area, not just their own, seemed like a worthwhile civic endeavour. True, there was an anti-statist strand running through the policy, but there was also a communitarian strand. It wasn't right-wing or left-wing – it transcended party politics.

This was reflected in my steering group, in which Labour and Lib Dem voters outnumbered Conservatives by two to one. When they heard the leaders of the teaching unions dismiss them as 'elitists', trying to set up a free school only because they were too snobbish or racist to send their children to the local community school, they were horrified. All of us, me included, wanted the West London Free School to be socially inclusive, reflecting the social and ethnic diversity of the area. We hadn't embarked on this project because we'd lost faith in the comprehensive ideal, but because we believed in it. During the 1964 general election campaign, when Labour was proposing to radically reform state education, Harold Wilson described comprehensives as 'grammar schools for all'. That's exactly what we wanted the West London Free School to be – a grammar school for all.

So why was the left so implacably opposed?

I bumped into Ed Miliband at a party shortly after he'd been elected leader and I asked him that question. 'Because it's robbing Peter to pay Paul,' he said. That's the nub of it, I think. But the belief that free schools will take money away from neighbouring schools is based on a misunderstanding. The budget for free schools comes from a separate funding stream to the budget for local authority-run schools, so more money for the former doesn't mean less for the latter. It's not a zero-sum game. In both cases, a school's revenue budget is calculated according to how many children are on the school's roll, and provided a new free school doesn't result in a neighbouring school becoming under-subscribed, the old school won't suffer any loss of revenue. Given how many additional school places we need to cope with England's growing population, it's unlikely that any state school is going to be under-subscribed as a result of a free school opening next door.

When I made this point to the Labour leader he mumbled something about 'capital costs', but that too is a straw man. The assumption here is that any capital funding provided to free schools is money that would otherwise be spent on refurbishing existing schools. This is the logic behind the BBC's habit of showing footage of comprehensives with leaking roofs whenever free schools are featured in the news. It's supposed to be an example of 'balanced' reporting. In fact, the basic need for more school places is so acute that if the government wasn't allocating capital funds to free schools it would be spending far more on creating new schools by more conventional methods. Under BSF, for instance, the average capital cost of setting up a new secondary school was £28 million. The total capital cost of setting up the first twenty-four free schools, by contrast, was £120 million – an average of £5 million per school. The truth is that in the absence of free schools there'd be even less money to spend on leaking roofs.

Miliband remained unconvinced – 'It's robbing Peter to pay Paul,' he repeated as he backed away – and he's not alone. Scarcely a day passes without somebody calling me a c*** on Twitter. This peaked in September 2010, when BBC2 broadcast a documentary about my free-school group. 'Anyone keen for some direct action against the new free schools (or against Toby Young, personally)?' tweeted a member of the Socialist Workers' Party during the broadcast. Well, yes, actually, there was. 'I don't think there's been one person yet on Toby Young's BBC2 documentary about starting a school that I wouldn't happily punch to death,' tweeted Marc Haynes, a BBC disc jockey. That was a bit alarming, considering my four young children were featured throughout.

I lay in bed that night unable to sleep. 'It's funny,' I said to Caroline. 'As a self-obsessed, celebrity journalist, I wasn't exactly universally loved, but it's only since setting out to do something genuinely worthwhile and public-spirited that I've became truly hated.'

*

The fact that the enemies of the policy were watching us like hawks meant my group couldn't afford to put a foot wrong. I don't just mean we had to avoid saying anything that could be used against us in the press. I mean we had to make sure we didn't do anything that could be challenged in the courts. The opponents of Blair's city academies were constantly bringing lawsuits against academy sponsors who hadn't crossed every 't' and dotted every 'i'. I had no doubt they'd use the same tactics against us if we gave them an opening.

We were advised by academy sponsors who'd been through this mill that the safest thing was to follow the standard set-up process, but there was no process. Before the change of government, academy sponsors had to tack their applications for funding on to the back of the applications submitted by their local authorities. We no longer had to do that – great, fantastic – but it wasn't clear what we were supposed to do instead. The difficulty we faced was that we were the first free-school group to submit a proposal to Michael Gove and, at that stage, he and his officials hadn't had time to put a new process in place.

We quickly discovered ourselves in a kind of bureaucratic maze – a maze designed by Escher. We would try to work our way through the labyrinth as best we could, but the ground kept shifting beneath our feet. Part of the problem was that the legal and regulatory framework we were supposed to be staying within was constantly evolving. We were told we must follow the rules – that was vitally important – but no one seemed to know what they were. There were various fixed points to navigate by – Acts of Parliament, High Court judgments, EU rules, etc. – but the language in which they are written – official, legalistic, precise – is misleading. These documents are both internally inconsistent and mutually inconsistent. At the margins, no two people agree on what is and isn't allowed. Everything is subject to interpretation.

'We're making it up as we go along,' said a senior civil servant when I vented my frustration. In some ways that was quite exciting. As the pathfinders, we could help create the process that other free-school groups would follow. But it was also nerve-wracking because without any clear guidelines about how to proceed we were more vulnerable to legal challenge.

In the middle of 2010 we switched our base of operations to the London Borough of Hammersmith and Fulham – a much friendlier council than Ealing – but I still felt like Sisyphus trying to push his giant rock up the hill. As the leader of the group, I had to familiarize myself with every aspect of the process: the ministers and their special advisors, the Free Schools Directorate, the Academies Set-Up Project Management Company Framework, the Outline Business Case, the Funding Agreement, the internal politics of the Children's Services Department of Hammersmith and Fulham. Then there's the army of educational consultancies and agencies, all professing to have expertise within one of several dozen fields: literacy, inclusion, SEN, SEAL, EAL, EBD. (It doesn't take long to run into an acronym storm.) As for the property side, there are the contractors, the technical advisors, the architects, the planners, the chartered surveyors, the quantity surveyors. The Education Funding Agency. The *Building Bulletins* – don't get me started on the *Building Bulletins*.

I remember coming across a passage in F. Scott Fitzgerald's *The Last Tycoon* in July of 2010 in which he describes his hero, the Hollywood studio chief Monroe Stahr, as being one of the few people in the business capable of keeping 'the whole equation' in his head.

I couldn't keep the whole equation in my head.

The words of Sandy Nuttgens, the leader of the parent group who set up the Elmgreen School in Lambeth, kept coming back to me: 'For four years I felt like I was on a vertical learning curve.'

Yet in spite of the mind-boggling complexity of it all, I now had the bit between my teeth. I was committed. I'd got this far with my merry little band and, God help me, I was going to go the whole way.

On 9 September 2011 Thomas Packer and I were waiting anxiously by the school gates, checking our watches every thirty seconds. Tom, a fifty-three-year-old retired commander in the Royal Naval Reserve and former head of a successful public school, had been appointed headmaster of the West London Free School nine months earlier and he'd been working tirelessly with our volunteer group to make sure we were ready to open. So far, so good. We'd secured a site, recruited eleven members of staff and filled all the places in the school. Indeed, at that very moment 120 eleven-year-olds were lining up in the hall in their smart new uniforms ready to sing 'Wade in the Water', which they'd been frantically rehearsing. The school had been open for forty-eight hours at this point, but this was the day of our opening ceremony. Boris Johnson was due to arrive at 9.30 a.m. so he could unveil our Founders' Plaque and officially declare the West London Free School open.

In the event, he was only fifteen minutes late, which

must be a record for Boris. The whole ceremony went off without a hitch – even our hastily cobbled-together curtain-pulling mechanism worked. Also present were the Mayor of Hammersmith and Fulham, the Mayor of Ealing, a couple of MPs, the Leader of the Council and numerous councillors and officials, not to mention the parents of all the children. They sat there, beaming away, as Boris gave a typically brilliant speech – entirely made up on the spot. He praised our school as one of the first free schools to be set up by a group of parents and expressed the hope that other groups of volunteers would follow in our footsteps. He paid particular tribute to the Secretary of State for Education and said he'd added a new inflection to the verb 'to give': we give, they gave, he gove.

'He gove us this fantastic new school,' he said. '*Floreat* the West London Free School.'

Had I told Jonathan Fingerhut that we'd have our school open within two years, he never would have believed me. It was just as well we managed it because I'm not sure I would have been able to hold my group together if it had taken any longer. Apart from everything else, they quickly grew tired of being bossed around by me and by September of 2011 a *coup d'état* was brewing. A year longer and they would have thrown me under a bus. The fact that Jonathan managed to keep his group together and remain at the helm for ten years is testimony to his extraordinary tenacity and diplomatic skills.

That we managed to pull it off was largely down to the hard work of the volunteer group and the support of Hammersmith and Fulham Council and the Department for Education. I'd started out with all the usual preconceptions about pettifogging bureaucrats and they certainly took a bit of getting used to, but by the end I'd grown to love them. The key was to get past the patrician mask and establish a personal bond. 'They're human beings,' one academy sponsor told me. 'Once you've made a connection you'll be surprised by how much they're willing to do to help.' Wise words.

Unlike Jonathan, I did feel it had all been worth it when I looked out and saw the faces of the children at our opening ceremony. I've written an international best-seller, performed in a one-man show in the West End and co-produced a Hollywood movie, but nothing I've ever done has come close to producing the sense of pride I felt on that day. What had started out as a project had become a crusade and I was standing in Jerusalem. We'd done it, by God. We'd founded one of England's first free schools and, with a bit of luck, started a revolution.

It's a ghastly, frustrating, time-consuming, mind-boggling business, but it's the best thing you'll ever do.

Welcome to the movement.

1

The Chicago Way

On 14 January 2011 the *Daily Mirror* ran a story headlined: 'Poor kids snubbed by new "bankers' school" set up with public cash.' The gist of it is contained in the following two paragraphs:

> Pupils from a struggling primary that lies on a deprived council estate have been told there will be no place for them at a ConDem free school being set up with backing from City fatcats.
>
> Yet those at four others in wealthier parts of the same area have been singled out as feeders for Bolingbroke Academy – dubbed the bankers' school – when it opens next year.

As you might expect, there's more to this story than meets the eye. The reason the proposers of this particular free school hadn't named the 'struggling primary' as one of the feeders is because they didn't want to disrupt the admissions of Battersea Park School, the secondary that pupils at the primary usually transferred to. Moreover, the primary in question isn't 'struggling' at all. It's called Falconbrook and in 2011 it was ranked 'good with outstanding features' by Ofsted.

The story originated with the GMB, a trade union that has been at the forefront of the opposition to the coalition's public-service reforms. At one point, the GMB even sent a couple of activists to stand outside Falconbrook to campaign against the free school, seemingly on behalf of the primary that had been so unfairly 'snubbed'. When a member of staff emerged from the school gates to ask them what they were doing – the headmistress wasn't particularly happy about her school being described as 'struggling' – they ran off. Subsequent calls to the GMB's headquarters from the school went unreturned.

It was the GMB, too, that 'dubbed' the Bolingbroke Academy 'the bankers' school'. One of the union's activists went through a petition on Wandsworth Council's website objecting to a planning application that had been submitted outlining an alternative use for the Bolingbroke Hospital, the site of the new school. He discovered that twenty-five of the signatories had some connection to the banking industry – a tiny fraction, given that over 600 people signed the petition. Remember, this was a petition objecting to an alternative use for the Bolingbroke site, not a petition endorsing the new school. Nevertheless, that was deemed sufficient grounds by the GMB – and, in turn, the *Daily Mirror* – to brand the Bolingbroke Academy a 'bankers' school' being set up by 'city fatcats'.

This is an example of the sort of abuse that most free-school proposers can expect at some point. It's important to remember that your opponents won't be constrained by such old-fashioned concepts as 'truth' and 'decency'. They will traffic in smears and misinformation, often resorting to downright lies. If you challenge their allegations publicly, they will furiously counter-attack. In private they will quote *The Godfather* at you: 'It's not personal. It's strictly business.' And politics, as you will discover, is a dirty business.

Some free-school proposer groups are reluctant to engage in the rough and tumble of political warfare. When a trade unionist or a local councillor tosses some calumny their way they keep their heads down and don't react in the hope that the story will disappear. They're anxious to appear 'apolitical' and worry that if they produce a robust response to the anti- campaign it will make them look like Tories. Above all, they want to avoid controversy. They're more comfortable flying below the radar.

This is a mistake. I cannot stress that strongly enough. Like all schools, your free school will stand or fall on its reputation. If you allow it to be branded a 'bankers' school' or similar, you're going to struggle to fill it once it's open. Parents will be put off by the bad publicity. Teachers will be reluctant to come and work for you. If you're going to have a chance of surviving, you need to take responsibility for defining your school from the beginning. You have to make sure *you* determine how your school is perceived, not your opponents. If you surrender that territory without a fight – which is what you'll be doing if you don't respond to their negative propaganda – you might as well abandon the whole project.

So you have to fight back. Every time a damaging story about your proposed new school appears in a newspaper or on the internet, you need to respond immediately. Create a Google alert with the name of your school so you know about any story the moment it appears. It doesn't matter what time of day it is, the rebuttal has to be instantaneous.

Let me give you an example. I remember sitting down one Sunday lunchtime to tuck into a roast with my wife and four children when I discovered that Fiona Millar, ex-advisor to Cherie Blair, had just written a post for an anti-free-schools website accusing my group of trying to throw some handicapped children out of their special school so we could move into the building. Not true, obviously, but I had to get up from the dinner table that second, go to my garden office, and spend the next two hours composing a 'comment' to leave beneath her piece that rebutted every element of the story. If I hadn't done that – and if I hadn't used the phrase 'false and malicious', indicating that the piece in question gave me ample ammunition to bring a libel suit against anyone repeating the allegations – the story could have ended up in the following day's *Mirror*.

The only way to win the propaganda war is to be every bit as energetic and relentless as your opponents. In some cases, more so. Whenever I talk to free-school proposer groups on this topic I like to quote another bit of dialogue from a movie, in this case, *The Untouchables*:

> You wanna know how to get Capone? They pull a knife, you pull a gun. He sends one of yours to the hospital, you send one of his to the morgue. *That's* the *Chicago* way and that's how you get Capone.

The Elevator Pitch

As soon as you go public with your proposal to set up a free school you need a pithy, one-sentence description of your school that captures its essence. For instance, the Reach Academy in Feltham, a free school being set up by a group of idealistic young teachers that's due to open in 2012, announces itself on its website as follows: 'Our vision is that all children, regardless of background, benefit from a first-class education and realize their full potential.' The free school being set up in Newham by Peter Hyman, a former strategy advisor for Tony Blair, is described as follows: 'School 21: For success in the 21st century.'

These are good examples of what's known in the business world as 'the elevator pitch' – a brief, punchy description of your idea that conveys its essence in thirty seconds or less. Free-school proposers often spend a lot of time on their 'Mission Statements' – longer descriptions of the values and objectives of the school's founders. These might serve some useful internal purpose, but they're useless when it comes to marketing your school. For that, you need something short and pithy.

Once you've decided on your 'elevator pitch', get it out there. Stick it on your website. Include it in all your campaign literature. Make sure that all the members of your group memorize it and trot it out at every available opportunity. This is how you win a political argument: you repeat the same thing over and over again. It's boring – it's one of the reasons politicians often give the impression of being slightly robotic – but you've got to do it. Your enemies know this and they're good at it. I loathe the GMB for branding the Bolingbroke Academy a 'bankers' school', but I tip my hat to their political acumen. It's an effective phrase and it's got so much traction I've heard it repeated on the *Today* programme. Indeed, the school has now changed its admissions policy to include Falconbrook as one of the feeder primaries in spite of the disruption this will cause to the neighbouring secondary school. One–nil to the GMB.

Staying On Message

In a sense, it wasn't a fair fight. The GMB is a well-oiled political machine: decisions are made, orders are given, discipline is imposed. Most free-school groups, by contrast, are reluctant to organize themselves too hierarchically. Not surprising, because it will inevitably involve some tension unless there's complete consensus about who should be in charge. Groups don't want to risk splintering into different factions so they will usually opt for a committee style of leadership, with decisions being taken collectively. Another reason it's difficult to impose a rigid chain of command is because no one's being paid. You can't ring up a voluntary worker in the middle of the night and order him or her to have a piece of work on your desk first thing tomorrow morning. He or she will tell you to get lost.

Nevertheless, when it comes to communications someone has to be in charge. Your group will need to respond immediately to a negative publicity hit and there won't be time to convene a meeting of 'the steering committee'. Not only that, but you need to make sure that the lines going out to the media are consistent – you need to stay 'on message'. Making sure that every member of the group says exactly the same thing when talking to the press or posting in a web forum is impossible – they're all going to give it their own little twist and, in the process, muddy the waters. Far easier if just one person is responsible for coms. That means no one apart from that person ever gives a quote to a newspaper, talks on the radio or makes any media appearance in connection with your school.

The risk of allowing more than one person to be a spokesperson for your group is that it increases the probability of error. Mastering the politics of free schools is difficult and what may strike one member of your group as a perfectly innocent, off-the-cuff remark could easily turn out to be something your enemies can exploit to discredit your school. It's a minefield, basically: one misstep and your whole project could be blown sky high. But that isn't a reason not to engage with your enemies or talk to the media. I repeat, that's not an option. Rather, it's a reason why one person and one person only should be entrusted with coms.

Andrew Adonis

From the outset, I decided to make the campaign for the West London Free School as public as possible. I wrote about it whenever I could and never hesitated to appear on radio or television to talk about it, often engaging in heated debates with Fiona Millar. The upshot was that our group, and me in particular, became the focus of national opposition to the free-schools policy, with the leaders of all the main teaching unions singling me out for criticism, not to mention Ed Balls, Andy Burnham and God knows who else. Whenever I bumped into other free-school proposers during the set-up process, they would often thank me for being their 'human shield'.

Not everyone on my steering group thought this was

the right approach and they weren't afraid to tell me so. They worried that people might think the West London Free School was just one big ego trip for its publicity-crazed founder or, worse, a Tory school. Often the Labour and Lib Dem voters on the steering group were just freaked out by being under attack from people they thought of as being on the same side as them. When I hit back, branding our opponents 'loony lefties', they were embarrassed. They thought this Punch-and-Judy style of debate was sophomoric and would mean our school wouldn't be taken seriously.

I began to doubt whether I'd made the right call myself and when I appeared on *Any Questions?* with Andrew Adonis I decided to seek his advice. This was just after the last general election. He kindly agreed to share a car with me back to London and I told him I was having second thoughts about dealing with my opponents so aggressively. A more helpful approach might be to invite them to meet with my group and see if we could find some common ground. Perhaps ask Fiona Millar what admissions policy she would regard as 'fair'. At bottom, we all wanted the same thing, which was good local schools for everyone, so it should be possible to engage in a constructive dialogue about how best to achieve that.

He gave me a look of withering contempt, much like the look Prospero gives his naive daughter in *The Tempest* when she expresses admiration for the rogues that have washed up on his island.

'They're not interested in "constructive dialogue",' he said. 'Don't you get it? If you extend any sort of olive branch to them they'll see it as a sign of weakness and move in for the kill. I dealt with exactly the same people – the Socialist Workers' Party, the Anti-Academies Alliance, the NUT – for most of my ministerial career and, believe me, they would rather stick pins in their eyes than admit they have common ground with someone like you. Their attitude to free schools is the same as their attitude to academies: they won't rest until every last one has been razed to the ground.'

I decided to stick to my guns and I'm convinced it was the right strategy. The acid test was when we advertised for staff in the *Times Educational Supplement*. Would any teachers want to work at 'the Toby Young school'? The answer was yes. We had over 600 applicants for our eight full-time teaching positions, including 120 for the job of head teacher. We've never had any problem attracting pupils, either. We received 1,074 applications for our second batch of 120 places making the West London Free School the most over-subscribed state secondary in Hammersmith and Fulham.

The War Room

If you want to know how to mount an effective political campaign, rent *The War Room* on DVD. It's a documentary that takes a behind-the-scenes look at Bill Clinton's 1992 presidential campaign. The star of the film is James Carville, Clinton's campaign manager and a supreme master of the dark political arts.

Among Carville's litany of pithy phrases, one of my favourites is the battle cry he always utters at the beginning of a campaign: 'Follow me if I advance, kill me if I retreat, avenge me if I die.'

I'm afraid that's the kind of martial attitude you've got to take when it comes to dealing with your opponents. By all means try and give the impression that you're reasonable people who would gladly engage in 'constructive dialogue' with them if only they were a little less ideologically hidebound – but only as a tactic to discredit them, obviously. In reality, don't give an inch. No retreat, no surrender. It's a battle to the death and there can only be one winner.

2

Location, Location, Location

Whenever a free-school proposer group gets in touch with me seeking advice, the first question I ask is, 'Have you got a site?' They often say 'yes', but nine times out of ten they haven't, not really. What they've got is some fantasy about converting an eighteenth-century Palladian mansion, even though it's a Grade I listed building. Or a scheme to erect a four-storey building with a 1,000-square-metre footprint on Metropolitan Open Land. Or some half-baked notion of buying a disused primary school from the local council, even though it's bitterly opposed to free schools. (My group indulged in all of the above fantasies at one point or another.) Finding a suitable site is the biggest obstacle you'll face in the course of setting up your school because they're as rare as hen's teeth, particularly in London. If you've got one – a real one, not some pipe dream – you're halfway there. If you haven't, you'd better start looking.

Curiously, not having a site isn't a deal breaker when it comes to getting approved. To get the green light from the Secretary of State – in reality, one of the approval panels set up by him – you need to fill out a lengthy application form setting out your ethos, curriculum, 'evidence of demand', business plan, etc. You're supposed to include *something* about your proposed location in your application, but plenty of free schools have been given the thumbs up without any site to speak of. I think the reason for this is that if Michael Gove only approved those groups that had clear, practical ideas about where to locate their schools the numbers would be embarrassingly small. Instead, he's instructed the approval panels to give more weight to other aspects of the proposals, such as the educational vision, in the hope that his officials can help the good ones find suitable sites.

Don't be lulled into a false sense of security by this. Without a site you're going to be hard pushed to open your school within twelve months of it being approved and any delay could be disastrous. (The groups approved to open schools in September 2013 were given the green light in July 2012, giving them fourteen months to D-Day.) Why is deferral a bad idea? Because more and more free schools are being approved each year and the longer you dilly-dally, the less money there'll be to go round. Worse, the coalition might have collapsed by the time you get round to applying for capital funding. So you need to have done some serious thinking about where you're going to put your school well in advance of submitting your application. Ideally, you should have a strategy for obtaining a site that you can start implementing as soon as you get the green light.

What follows is some general advice about where to locate your school. It's far from exhaustive. In particular, there's nothing about how many square metres you'll need per child or how it should be divided up between general teaching areas, science labs, circulation space, etc. (You can get all that information from the New Schools Network.) You should also bear in mind that you could probably ignore all this advice and still end up with a school. But if you want to maximize your chances of success, read on.

Basic Need

One of the distinctions you're going to have to get your head round is the difference between demand and basic need. Demand is the number of children that are likely to apply for places at your school once it's up and running, while basic need is the total number of children in the area who are currently without school places.

Now, the only thing you're asked to demonstrate in your free-school proposal is 'evidence of demand', not basic need. Petitions, emails, etc. (Again, the New Schools Network can give you chapter and verse on this.) In theory there could be surplus places in your area – that is, more school places than there are children of school age – and your free school could still get approved. But in the absence of basic need, the 'evidence of demand' will have to be pretty robust.

To understand this, you need to put yourself in Michael Gove's shoes. The last thing he wants is for one of the free schools he's approved to start failing – and number one on the risk register is a falling roll. Schools have high fixed costs and need to be operating close to full capacity to stay afloat. Once the number of children on roll falls below a certain magic number, they go into the red. If this happens to a local authority-run school, the council will usually pour resources in to try and turn things round. But a free school has no such safety net. If its roll starts to fall below a critical point, Michael Gove will be faced with a stark choice: he'll either have to bail it out or allow it to close. Both options would be politically disastrous. He would not have fun explaining either decision to John Humphrys at 8 a.m. on a Monday.

Consequently, the Secretary of State will have instructed his approval panels to apply a good deal of scrutiny to the 'evidence of demand' section in the applications. And the simple truth is that you'll be on much safer ground if you can demonstrate basic need, i.e. prove there's a genuine shortage of school places in the area you're proposing to put your school. If you can do that, you'll have gone some way towards allaying Michael Gove's fears. After all, if there's an acute need for additional school places, you're not going to have as much difficulty filling your roll than if there's a surplus of places. However, demonstrating basic need isn't all you'll need to do. The Department for Education (DfE) says on its website that one of the common failings of unsuccessful applications is that they only provide evidence of basic need without demonstrating that local parents specifically want the sort of school they're proposing. The key point is that in the absence of basic need the bar you'll need to get over will be that much higher.

There's another reason why basic need is a factor, which is that the Secretary of State has a political incentive to provide school places for children who need them. After all, if tens of thousands of four-year-olds are left without primary-school places each year, that's a lot of angry mums and dads. Same goes for eleven-year-olds. Michael Gove can do his best to blame local authorities, but they'll say their hands were tied by the cuts. At the end of the day, the buck stops with the Secretary of State. Consequently, he's going to be more inclined to approve those proposals for free schools located in areas of basic need than those that aren't. It's two birds with one stone – he's catering for basic need *and* pursuing an important policy objective at the same time. Contrast this with free schools being set up in areas where they're surplus to requirements. Not only will he have the problem of basic need to deal with, he'll have the additional difficulty of justifying why he's spending money on new schools in areas where they aren't needed and neglecting those where they are.

All of which is a roundabout way of saying that if you can locate your school in an area that has a demonstrable shortage of school places, your application is more likely to be approved. Of the forty primary free schools approved in July 2012, eighty-eight per cent were in areas that face a shortfall in primary places.

Social Deprivation

The same goes for social deprivation. When the first twenty-four free schools were unveiled in August 2011, a heated debate broke out about whether 50 per cent of them were in the lower half of the 'deprivation index' produced by the Department of Communities and Local Government (DCLG). The DfE claimed they were, the *Guardian* claimed they weren't. The argument turned on how the location of a school is defined. Is the relevant factor the school's postcode or its catchment area?

This is a sensitive point for the coalition because the enemies of the policy have had some success in branding free schools as 'middle-class vanity projects'. Nick Clegg in particular is anxious to dispel the impression that free schools are just going to be for the children of the well-off and gave a speech shortly after the first batch had been approved in which he urged Michael Gove to make sure the next batch were 'open to all children and not just the privileged few'. 'I want to see all of them in poorer neighbourhoods,' he said. 'Or in areas crying out for more school places.'

This was a piece of grandstanding by the Deputy Prime Minister, who has no direct influence over which free schools are given the thumbs-up. Nevertheless, if Michael Gove has to choose between two schools, the first of which is located in the bottom half of the 'deprivation index', the second of which is in the top, and both have scored the same on the approval panels' evaluation matrix, he's going to choose the former.

Officially, this is only supposed to be a 'contextual' consideration, a comparatively minor factor in the DfE's overall assessment of your application. But, as with basic need, there's a *dignified* version of the approvals process and an *efficient* version. The political reality is that if you're proposing to set up your school in a socially deprived area it has a higher chance of being approved. Of the eighty-five mainstream free schools approved in July 2012, sixty-seven per cent were in the lower half of the DCLG's deprivation index.

Make Sure the Council is Onside

In the Introduction I said how relieved my group was when the local authority veto was removed. That relief turned out to be short lived. In the course of setting up the West London Free School we discovered that a hostile council still has the power to obstruct a proposer group – one of the reasons we switched operations from Ealing to Hammersmith and Fulham. Unless the site you've got your eye on is already being used as a school of the same size and type as the one you're trying to set up, you're almost certainly going to have to get planning permission before you can open a school on that site. Even if the building already has D1 consent – health centre, museum, library, place of worship – you'll still need permission if you propose to change it in any way. And if the local authority is opposed to free schools, you're unlikely get it.

At one point it looked as though the government was going to liberalize the planning rules, making it possible for free schools to open in shops and offices without having to obtain 'change of use' consent. However, when it consulted local authorities about these proposals, the government ran into a wall of opposition. In response, the changes were watered down. Free-school proposers still have to get planning permission, the only concession being that councils are now supposed to make a 'presumption' in their favour. Disappointed petitioners can appeal to the DCLG and ask the Secretary of State to overturn the decision, but that's a laborious process and, in the interim, the site could be sold to someone else.

There are other advantages to having a sympathetic local authority. For one thing, it might be willing to sell you a site. Some proposer groups are lucky enough to have a relationship with a rich philanthropist who has agreed to give them a site, but the majority will be expecting the DfE to purchase a site on their behalf. Now, in theory it shouldn't matter whether the site in question is publicly or privately owned. The DfE's sole consideration should be getting the best possible deal for the taxpayer. But the reality is that the DfE will be more willing to buy the site if it's owned by the council rather than by a commercial property company. There are a number of reasons for this, but the main one is that public servants, whether politicians or bureaucrats, are more comfortable giving large sums of money to public bodies than private ones. It's keeping it in the family.

Another benefit of having the local authority onside is that it might be prepared to lease your group a temporary building while your permanent site is being made ready. You're probably not going to have time to get your main site up to scratch by the date you want to open your school, so you're going to need a temporary one. The council is more likely to have something suitable than any of the commercial property companies in your area – a disused primary school, for instance. It might even let you have the temporary site for nothing.

In the best-case scenario a friendly council will simply give your group a permanent site free of charge, particularly if you're proposing to set up a primary in an area desperately in need of more primary places. In those circumstances, you'll only be asking the DfE to pay for the refit of the building and it goes without saying that the lower the capital cost of your school, the more likely the Secretary of State is to approve it.

To illustrate the importance of having a well-disposed local authority, consider the fate of two different free schools, one in Wandsworth, the other in Lambeth.

Based in south Battersea, the Wandsworth group is

known as the NSC (Neighbourhood School Campaign) and it's been campaigning for a new secondary school in the area since 2009. In 2010 the group joined forces with ARK (Absolute Return for Kids), one of the most successful multi-academy sponsors, and together they submitted a proposal for a free school. It was one of the first proposals to be given the thumbs-up by the Secretary of State and, shortly afterwards, Wandsworth Council agreed to purchase Bolingbroke Hospital from the local NHS Trust and transfer the freehold to the free school. This is the 'bankers' school' referred to in the previous chapter and it's due to open in September 2012.

The group in Lambeth is led by Katharine Birbalsingh, the ex-deputy head teacher who hit the headlines when she told the 2010 Conservative Party Conference that standards in most state schools had fallen dramatically under the last government. Her group is hoping to establish the Michaela Community School, a secondary school with a traditional, academic curriculum that caters for all the children in the local area, particularly African-Caribbean boys. To begin with, the site Birbalsingh had her eye on was Lilian Baylis, a former secondary school in Kennington owned by Lambeth Council. Various bureaucrats from the DfE came and gave it the once over and agreed that, yes, it would make an excellent secondary school. The officials told the steering group that, provided the proposal was approved, the department would be minded to purchase the site on its behalf. So far, so good.

But Birbalsingh's group hadn't bargained on the opposition of Lambeth Council. In between the submission of the proposal in May 2011 and its approval in September, Lambeth agreed to sell Lilian Baylis to a commercial property developer. The fact that there's a need for a new secondary school in Lambeth, particularly one aimed at underachieving black boys, was neither here nor there. The council decided it would rather Lilian Baylis was turned into a block of flats – anything – than a free school.

The Michaela Community School was among the batch of sixty-five free schools to be approved in the second wave, but since it doesn't have a site the chances of it opening any time soon are pretty remote. When I last spoke to Katharine Birbalsingh she told me she'd given up hope of ever opening a free school in Lambeth and is now looking for a site in Wandsworth.

It so happens that Lambeth is Labour controlled and Wandsworth is Conservative controlled, but it would be wrong to conclude you'll always be better off trying to establish a free school in a Conservative local authority. There are some Labour councils that are well-disposed towards free schools – Manchester City Council, for instance – just as there are some Conservative ones that aren't. As I said in the Introduction, the unelected officials are usually the people calling the shots so the political complexion of the council is often irrelevant. It's the Town Hall Sir Humphreys you need to win over.

Consequently, the most useful piece of advice I can offer to anyone hoping to set up a free school is to make contact with your local authority. With a bit of luck, you'll manage to get a meeting with the lead member for children's services. He'll probably be quite friendly – he's a politician, after all – but the person you should pay attention to is the man at the back of the room taking notes (it's usually a man). He'll be an assistant director in the Children's Services Department and it's his boss, the

Director of Children's Services, who'll decide your fate. If the man is friendly – if he gives you any sign of encouragement, however subtle – chances are you'll end up with a free school. If he avoids eye contact and generally tries to remain inscrutable, you probably won't.

A Note on Leasing

One option many free-school groups consider is leasing a site from a commercial property company. This is something the DfE says it's prepared to consider. However, I wouldn't invest too much hope in this. For one thing, few companies will be willing to lease a site to a brand-new charitable trust with no credit history to speak of. You might find one or two prepared to take the risk, but they will build that risk into the price of the lease, thereby making it unaffordable.

There is a way round this, which is to persuade the DfE to guarantee your lease and, again, the department says it's willing to consider that. But it'll take a good deal of persuasion because the financial liability will then appear on the PSBR (Public Sector Borrowing Requirement). That never goes down well with the Treasury. As you may have noticed, the present government isn't keen on public sector borrowing.

There's also the issue of how you're going to pay the rent. A free school's annual revenue budget is calculated according to how many children are on the school's roll. Free schools get the same amount per capita as the equivalent state schools in the borough. Their annual revenue budgets don't include a little bit extra so they can lease buildings. Again, there's a way round this, which is to persuade the Secretary of State to give you an annual grant in addition to your revenue budget to cover the cost of your rent. But such arrangements are unusual.

Another difficulty is that most buildings require some refitting if they're going to be suitable for use as a school – even those that have already been used as schools at some point in their history – and that can run to many millions of pounds. The estimated cost of turning Bolingbroke Hospital into the Bolingbroke Academy, for instance, is over £10 million. Why would the DfE make that sort of investment if the building in question is being leased from a commercial property company?

I'm not saying the DfE won't help you lease a building under any circumstances, but you'll have a job convincing the officials that the combined cost represents better value for money than any of the alternatives. Or, indeed, good value for money in the absence of any alternative. Bear in mind that in the long term it's always going to be cheaper for the DfE to come up with an initial lump sum to purchase and refit a building than it is to pay an annual rent indefinitely.

3

The Swedish Model

In February of 2010 I had a strange experience during a trip to Sweden. Some members of the West London Free School steering group were visiting IES Eskilstuna, a free school about seventy-five miles from Stockholm. IES, which stands for Internationella Engelska Skolan, is the second-largest free-school chain in Sweden and the reason we'd made the 1,150-mile trip is because the company had expressed an interest in setting up some free schools in England.

We were being shown round by Damian Brunker, the academic manager of all the IES schools, and when we walked into the first classroom all the children leapt to their feet and said, 'God mórgon, Herr Brunker.' As they stood there, waiting to be given permission to sit down again, I noticed that they were assembled in rows behind neat wooden desks and that the teacher was standing at the front of the class clutching a piece of chalk. It was as if we'd stepped through a portal in space and time and found ourselves in a typical English grammar school in the 1950s. A form of education that fell out of fashion long ago in England – chalk and talk – had been reborn in the world's most progressive social democracy. How did this happen?

The short answer is free schools. The voucher system introduced by the centre-right coalition in 1992 broke up the state's monopoly over taxpayer-funded education and made it possible for independent operators to enter the sector, whether parent cooperatives or commercial chains like IES. This 'marketization' of Sweden's public education system resulted in a transfer of power away from education officials and towards parents, some of whom clearly prefer the traditional pedagogy of schools like IES Eskilstuna. Not surprising when you consider that IES has the best academic track record of all the school providers in Sweden, including 'municipal schools', in spite of having a fully comprehensive intake.

We were bowled over by the school – it was exactly what we wanted the West London Free School to be – and started talking to IES about a potential partnership. In many ways, the ideal solution would have been for the company simply to open a secondary school in Ealing without any involvement from a group of parents. But that wasn't an option. In Sweden, thanks to the reforming zeal of the 1992–4 government, it's possible for a commercial education provider to set up, own and operate a free school. Indeed, the largest free-school chain in Sweden – Kunskapsskolan, with thirty-two schools – is a for-profit company. But in Britain, the coalition has stopped short of allowing that. Of the 191 free-school proposals approved at the time of writing, all have been submitted by charitable trusts. Nick Clegg often claims credit for having reined in the free-market instincts of the Secretary of State, but Michael Gove never had any plans to enable for-profit companies to set up free schools. The Conservative Party leadership concluded long ago that to allow that in their first term would be a step too far. When Gove and others are tackled about this by right-wing Tory backbenchers they sometimes say they would have gone further if it hadn't been for those pesky Lib Dems, but that's just an excuse. The truth is, the Tories wouldn't have taken this step even if they'd won an overall majority, and it's far from certain that they'll take it even if they win one at the next election.

Why? Because there's a widespread feeling among the public that state education is sacrosanct and shouldn't be sullied by the profit motive. Never mind that for-profit companies are already embedded in the state sector – providing IT, carrying out Ofsted inspections, running school improvement services, etc. Many people think that allowing companies to profit from children's education is just wrong. In an electoral landscape in which both major parties have to battle for the centre ground, the Conservatives are wary of doing anything quite *that* controversial.

No, it was abundantly clear that if we wanted an IES school in our neighbourhood we would need to first establish ourselves as a charitable trust and then enter into some sort of partnership with the company.

The Hybrid

The Free School Applicant's Handbook, published by the New Schools Network, contains a section entitled 'Choosing a model' which compares three broad organizational structures: an applicant-run school in which the group applying to set up the free school is proposing to take complete responsibility for it; a sponsor-run school in which the group turns over complete responsibility to a non-profit education provider, such as a multi-academy sponsor; and a school-provider model in which the group applying to set up the school takes overall responsibility for it, but outsources the day-to-day running of the school to an education provider.

I'm going to talk about the first two in a later section, but it's the third option – the hybrid – that I want to discuss here. The interesting thing about this model is that the provider in question can be a commercial company. It doesn't have to be a charity. Consequently, if this is a viable model, it should be possible for a group like mine to go into partnership with a company like IES.

But is it?

The answer is yes, but it is fiendishly difficult. We sought legal advice and were told that, in theory, it was possible for a charitable trust to outsource the operation of a taxpayer-funded school to a third party. Indeed, there was a precedent. From 2007 to 2010 Turin Grove School, a local authority-run comprehensive in Enfield, entered into a contract with EdisonLearning, a commercial education provider, to manage the school.

But there were some hoops we'd need to jump through. Because taxpayers' money was involved, the education provider would have to be publicly procured – we couldn't just award the contract to IES – and there was a strict procedure we'd have to follow. This made sense, even though it involved a huge amount of work on our part. After all, IES might not be the best provider out there. We'd been impressed by the school we'd visited in Eskilstuna, but other schools run by different companies might be just as good. We had a duty, not just to the taxpayer, but to the parents and pupils of our prospective school, to be as diligent as possible.

Luckily, a couple of people in the steering group had some experience of letting contracts in the public sector and, with their help, we managed to tick most of the boxes. We put together a glossy-looking 'Invitation to Tender' and published a notice in the *Official Journal of the European Community* informing all interested parties of this opportunity, something we were required to do by EU procurement law.

The upshot was that we were deluged with proposals from all the usual suspects in the education field: Edison-Learning, CfBT, Cognita, GEMS, Nord Anglia, Serco and Kunskapsskolan, in addition to IES. We even had some unusual suspects: Collingwood, Creative Learning and Haberdashers' Aske's.

To help us sift through the proposals we put together an evaluation matrix and scored the different bids, coming up with a longlist of ten. Cue lots of visits to schools and a succession of meetings at which we cross-examined each of the bidders, trying to get a sense of which company would be the best fit.

Before shortlisting, I thought it would be prudent to ask the DfE's legal team if they would stand behind us in the event of a legal challenge by a disappointed bidder. Naturally, they wanted to know more about the procedure we'd followed so I turned over all the proposals to them, along with our evaluations and a detailed log of all the meetings we'd had.

After several weeks the DfE's lawyers got back in touch to say they thought the tender process we'd run was extremely professional – really very impressive. Unfortunately, it wasn't quite impressive enough. To be on the safe side, we ought to run the entire process again from scratch.

Christ on a bike!

It had taken six months of continual meetings to get to this point. Did we really have to go through all that again? And how would the bidders react if we asked them all to re-submit on the grounds that we'd cocked up first time round? It wouldn't exactly inspire confidence.

OK, I said. If we do agree to re-run the process, will you tell us what we did wrong the first time and advise us how to do it properly this time?

Oh no, they said. We couldn't possibly do that. It's not our place to tell you what to do. You've asked for our opinion about whether the process you've run is legally robust and we've given you our answer. Beyond that, we cannot comment.

At the time I thought they were being deliberately unhelpful because they disapproved of the free-schools policy, but on reflection I think they were as frustrated as we were by the lack of any tramlines for groups like ours to follow. Allowing volunteers to take over the running of public services, either on their own or in partnership with established providers, was the overarching theme of the Conservatives' election manifesto. That's what David Cameron meant by the 'Big Society' (at least, I think it was). But no government department, including the Department for Education at this point, had yet put any process in place to enable that to happen. As far as the DfE's lawyers were concerned, it was just a lot of hot air.

They did make one helpful suggestion, however. Why didn't we hire a firm of specialist procurement lawyers to oversee our tender? Indeed, they thought the DfE might even be prepared to cover our legal costs.

OK, now we were getting somewhere. If we did that and the specialists signed off on the tendering process, would the DfE's lawyers then be prepared to stand behind us in the event of a challenge?

Er, no. The official position was that if we wanted to press ahead and enter into a partnership with an established provider like IES, the DfE wouldn't stand in our way. But if we were challenged, we'd be on our own.

At this point I thought it would be prudent to consult our lawyer again. Just how great was the risk of being taken to court?

The news wasn't good. Not only was there a risk of being challenged by a disappointed bidder, a risk that we could mitigate but not eliminate by re-running the process, there was also a risk of being challenged by a politically motivated individual put up to it by one of the militant left-wing groups that oppose free schools.

After the lawyer had given our group his advice we stayed up long into the night debating what to do. Should we take the risk? After assessing all the bids we were still pretty impressed by IES and the prospect of ending up with an IES school was appealing. But what if there was a legal challenge? The DfE had not offered to indemnify us and, in all likelihood, we wouldn't be able to fund a protracted legal action, no matter how great our chances of success. Our opponents would probably know this and, as a consequence, be even more likely to come after us in the courts. The prospect of being beggared by a lawsuit, followed by a humiliating capitulation when the coffers ran dry, wasn't particularly appealing.

There were other arguments against the hybrid. We were concerned that entering into a partnership with a third party might make it harder to attract a good head. By this time, I'd recruited John McIntosh, an ex-headmaster of the London Oratory School, to the steering group. The idea of having to report to the school's board of governors *and* the board of an external education company was anathema to him. We were impressed by John, a figure of towering authority, and we'd made up our minds to recruit a head exactly like him if we could. That meant someone wise and level-headed, but also strong-willed and independent. A sort of Philosopher King. If John was put off by the prospect of having to report to two boards, other good heads would be too.

Then there was the money. The only reason the companies had submitted bids is because they thought they could make money out of operating our school – that is, they believed they could run the school for less than the DfE would give us to run the school. And that applied to the charities as well as the for-profits. Didn't matter whether the resulting saving was called a 'profit' or a 'surplus', it was money that wouldn't be spent on the kids at our school. When we raised this doubt with the bidders they all said the same thing, namely, that they could deliver more for 90p than we could for a pound, thanks to economies of scale. But could they? Or would the head teacher end up on the phone to the provider each day, begging for more textbooks?

As I weighed all this up, it dawned on me that the reason I'd been so keen to enter into a partnership with an education company is because I was finding the whole set-up process a bit overwhelming. I thought an experienced provider could take the heavy lifting off my hands. I fantasized about assuming a more strategic role, surveying the field of battle from my vantage point on a hilltop rather than grubbing about in the mud.

But after spending so much time shuttling back and forth to the DfE, talking to lawyers, visiting schools and doing due diligence on various education companies, I now felt more confident. I was developing a feel for navigating my way through the murk. I've always been a great believer in the principle that if you want something done right you have to do it yourself and the prospect of relinquishing control to a third party, however impressive, was becoming less and less attractive.

After a lengthy deliberation, we decided to go it alone.

Is a Hybrid Possible?

Some parent groups imagine they'll only have to procure a provider if the company in question is a commercial entity. Not so. Procurement rules apply whether the company is for-profit or non-profit. I've come across groups who believe they can get round the legal obligation to run a public procurement process by forming a joint venture with a charitable provider before applying for approval, so the proposal takes the form of a joint application. They think that, post-approval, the charity in question can then just be awarded the contract to operate the school. That won't work. If the joint venture entered into by the parent group and the charity to take overall responsibility for the school is a separate legal entity to the charity, the charity's services will have to be procured in the normal manner – it cannot simply be awarded the contract with no competition. The only way round this is if the charity alone, rather than the notional joint venture, applies to set up the school. But in that case, the model would not be a hybrid. It would be a sponsor-run school.

I know of one example of a hybrid school – the Breckland Free School in Suffolk. The parent group, having first formed a charitable trust and with their application approved, were then able to subcontract the management of Breckland to a third party – IES, as it happens. But the reason they could do this is because the procurement process was run by the DfE's Finance and Commercial Division as a pilot scheme and, at the time of writing, the department hasn't put a permanent process in place on the back of this. That may change, of course, and you should check with the New Schools Network for the latest news.

The Other Two Models

As with leasing a building, it's theoretically possible to make the hybrid model work and it wouldn't be a deal breaker as far as an approval panel is concerned. You're just unlikely to get very far once your school has been given the green light. After our aborted attempt to outsource the management of the West London Free School, I concluded that the only way it could work would be if the DfE put a process in place to enable proposer groups to procure the services of education providers in a risk-free way. That would mean setting up a procurement framework and legally indemnifying all the participants. Nothing to stop the Secretary of State asking his officials to do that, but I'm doubtful it will happen in the lifetime of this Parliament. For one thing, it would look like a sneaky way to allow for-profits to run free schools – privatization by the back door. For another, Michael Gove just doesn't like procurement frameworks. Too bureaucratic.

Generally speaking, you're much better off going for one of the other two options: an applicant-run school or a sponsor-run school.

The first of these is the purest. No fussing about with third parties. Your proposer group forms itself into a charitable trust, submits an application and, if it's successful, sets up a school. That means you get to design the uniform, decide on the admissions policy, draw up the school policies, etc. All the decisions, big and small, will be taken by you – at least until you appoint the head teacher, which, incidentally, is the most important decision your group will ever make. A majority of the people on your steering group will go on to become governors of the school and they're the ones who'll be in overall charge going forward. If the head teacher turns out to be crap, it'll be their job to fire him or her and recruit a better one. It's an awesome amount of responsibility – and a considerable amount of work – but at least your group will retain control. That's what we decided to do at the West London Free School and I think it was the right decision.

However, there is an alternative – a sponsor-run school. I stumbled across this model by accident when my group was considering the bids that had been submitted from various education providers in response to our notice in the *Official Journal of the European Community*. I noticed that none of the multi-academy sponsors had been in touch and decided to approach ARK and Harris – by common consent, the best in the business – to see if either of them might be interested in a partnership with us.

The answer was 'maybe', but only if we were happy for them to take over the entire project lock, stock and barrel. That is to say, it would be them, not us, who submitted an application to the DfE; them, not us, who signed a Funding Agreement with the Secretary of State; and them, not us, who took responsibility for the school hereafter. In short, they were only willing to consider working with us if we ceded complete control to them. The most my group could hope for would be a couple of seats on the governing body. Not exactly a partnership, then.

That's a sponsor-run school. It's no different from the academies set up by ARK and Harris under the previous government. The parent group might have a role on the marketing side, trying to drum up custom and so forth, but beyond that not much input.

Given how much of a control freak I am, that didn't appeal to me. Nevertheless, it does appeal to some other groups. A woman called Emily Philips started a campaign for a new free primary school in Shepherd's Bush and her group ended up throwing in its lot with ARK. The result was the ARK Conway Primary Academy, one of the first free schools to open in 2011.

If you're thinking about going into partnership with one of the multi-academy sponsors, your best hope of exerting some control is by holding a beauty parade beforehand, inviting all the big players to come and strut their stuff in your sitting room. Some of them will be keen to work with you, if only because their application is more likely to be approved if you're involved. That means you can extract concessions from them, maybe even demand an equal number of seats on the governing body. Problem is, the sponsors willing to make a deal like that will probably be on the crappy side. Make sure you go and visit some of the schools they're already funding before getting into bed with them – not just the schools they suggest you visit, but the ones they don't want you to see as well. Chances are, that's what your school will end up being like.

Bear in mind that once you've handed over control there'll be no going back. They can renege on all their promises and there'll be nothing you can do about it. So you should make sure that what the sponsor does already is exactly what you want.

Your Children

The biggest concern most parent groups will have about turning over their beloved projects to multi-academy sponsors is that their children won't be given priority in the admissions process once the school opens. Indeed, I know of one parent group who were reassured by a multi-academy sponsor that their children would be a shoo-in, only to have the sponsor tell them later that such favouritism wasn't possible because the School Admissions Code of Practice forbade it. That's not entirely honest. It is indeed forbidden by the Admissions Code, but a free school can include an annex in its Funding Agreement – Annex B – whereby the Secretary of State allows the school to circumvent the Admissions Code in certain respects. Giving priority to the children of parent-founders is one such example. Michael Gove accepts that you can't expect parents to do all the work required to set up a free school without offering them something in return. For most of us, making sure our children have a decent school to go to is the main motive and the current Secretary of State recognizes that. So if you do hand over to a multi-academy sponsor, make sure they're signed up to this. And don't take a sponsor's word for it. Get it in writing.

4

The Application Process

In the run-up to the 2010 general election, I used to joke with Lesley Surman, one of the leaders of a free-school group in Kirklees, about which of us would be first to get our proposal on Michael Gove's desk. We both thought it was important to be first out of the blocks, not least because we suspected we'd soon have plenty of competitors. That turned out to be right. By the end of 2010, the New Schools Network had received over 700 queries from groups interested in setting up free schools.

Unfortunately, neither of us could get going as fast as we wanted. We had to wait six weeks just for the DfE to produce the application form. The good news was that when the form eventually materialized it wasn't too onerous. My group had no trouble answering the first question – 'Is your local authority aware of your intention to set up a free school?' – and filling in the rest of it was just a matter of cutting and pasting from our campaign literature. There was a section asking for 'evidence of demand' (see Chapter 2), but you were told to limit your answer to 200 words.

Once our proposal had been approved, we were asked to fill in a second form inviting us to tick a series of boxes indicating those areas in which we needed the most help. ('Is there a box that says "All of the Above"?' I joked.) This was used by the DfE to create an 'Invitation to Tender' that was then distributed to all the firms on its project-management company framework. About half a dozen bids came in and we spent an afternoon evaluating them in the company of two officials at the DfE. (The proposer group chooses the firm, but the contractor is the DfE.) E. C. Harris's bid scored highest and not long afterwards we were assigned a project manager in the form of Louise Allanach, one of the company's equity partners.

Louise was a godsend. By common consent, she is the best project manager in the academies set-up field. She's an elegant Scotswoman in her mid-thirties whose silky smooth exterior conceals a steel-trap mind. With her help, we spent the next few months putting together an Outline Business Case (OBC), addressing the same questions asked in the application form but in more detail. The main document ran to thirty-four pages and there were eighteen appendices. Only after our OBC had been approved did we move to the 'pre-opening stage' and I'm not sure we would have got there without Louise's help.

The New Process

When my group applied to open a primary in 2013, the bar was a lot higher. Instead of first submitting a proposal and then following up with an OBC, we had to submit a document that sat somewhere between the two. It didn't have to be a fully fledged OBC, but it had to contain a lot more detail than our initial application. For example, instead of just 200 words on 'evidence of demand', Section E of the form asked for proof that there was sufficient demand to fill all the places in the first two years of the school's life. That meant securing explicit commitments from the parents of more than 120 children, stating that our school would be their first preference in 2013 and 2014. No easy task.

But the key difference is that we weren't eligible for any funding until this more detailed application had been approved. So there was no project manager on hand to help prepare our case. For us, that wasn't too onerous because we'd already been through the process once, but there were plenty of proposers that couldn't get over this new, higher bar. Over 250 groups applied to set up schools in the third wave and less than half were approved to go to the next stage.

There are several reasons why the DfE has tightened up the process – and I don't imagine it will get any easier from now on. For one thing, any group capable of getting over the bar is more likely to be adept at running a school, thereby reducing the risk of failure. (Section F of the 2013 application form was entitled 'Capacity and capability'.) There's also a financial consideration. Once the schools have been approved, there's less for project managers to do so there's been a commensurate drop in the funds made available to successful proposer groups. All perfectly understandable.

But the indirect consequence of raising the bar and reducing the funds available for project-management support is that it's harder for parent groups like mine to get through the process. The playing field is now tilted in favour of companies like E-Act, the multi-academy sponsor that was, until recently, run by Sir Bruce Liddington, a former civil servant at the DCSF. In 2011 Sir Bruce announced his intention to create a 'super-chain' of 250 free schools. It's beginning to look as though a policy designed to shift the balance of power away from the state and towards volunteer groups has been hijacked by the professionals.

Nevertheless, there are ways to improve your chances of success, some of which I shall now discuss.

Recruit Experts

I recently asked Fran Sims, our 'project lead' at the DfE on the first school, whether it had been a bit of a shock for her having to deal with a bunch of amateurs like us. 'But you aren't really amateurs,' she said. She's right. We were almost all middle-class professionals. We might not have set up a secondary school before, but the group included an ex-headmaster of one of the best comprehensives in the country, the director of academic management at a leading independent school, a retired special-needs teacher and several school governors. On the property side, we had two architects, a chartered surveyor, a quantity surveyor and a planning consultant. As an experienced journalist, I was able to handle the media and then there was my wife Caroline, who's a solicitor. We even had a senior civil servant on the team to act as a sort of interpreter when it came to talking to DfE officials. The only thing we lacked was an accountant. Our business plan was written by a music-industry executive and an economist at Ofgem.

There's no denying that we were an unusually well-qualified group. One criticism of free schools – and of the

Big Society in general – is that you need this sort of expertise to stand a chance of success and less well-connected people don't have access to it. I'm not so sure about that. Apart from my wife, the only person in my group I knew beforehand was the music-industry executive. Of the rest, some contacted me out of the blue, others were people I brought on board after meeting them in another context, while the rest were introduced by the existing members of the group. Assembling this team wasn't difficult. On the contrary, I was deluged with emails on a daily basis by experts offering to help. I could easily have replicated my group three or four times over.

Once word gets out that you're trying to set up a free school, your difficulty won't be in recruiting people with the requisite expertise, but fending them off. My advice is to choose the team carefully, making sure the people you end up with are willing to make the necessary time commitment. Pay close attention to the application form on the DfE's website and ensure you have a person on your team capable of filling out each of the different sections. For 2013 openers, that meant an expert in each of the following fields: setting up a company (lawyer), articulating the group's educational vision (teacher), drawing up an educational plan (ex-headmaster/senior teacher), providing 'evidence of demand' (demographer/market researcher), demonstrating organizational capability (entrepreneur/company director), assessing potential sites (architect/chartered surveyor/quantity surveyor/property consultant) and writing a business plan (businessman/economist). In some cases, you can entrust a particular work stream to more than one person, but it's a good idea not to have more than one representative from any single profession. (If we hadn't had two architects in our group we could have avoided a lot of arguments.) In addition, you need someone willing to take on all the admin – arrange meetings of the steering group, send out reminders, circulate agendas, keep minutes, etc. If that person also has some desktop publishing skills, so much the better.

Professional Help

If my experience is anything to go by, you'll also be contacted by several commercial companies offering to do some pro bono work. For the most part, these will be education providers and/or project-management companies. The reason they're offering to help, of course, is that they're hoping your group will be in a position to give them some paid work down the line.

Now, as I explained in the previous chapter, the prospects of making any sort of hybrid model fly at the moment are slim, so there's little hope of your ever being in a position to award a contract to an education provider. Of course, the provider-in-question may not be aware of that and you might be tempted to exploit that naivety in order to get them to do some of the heavy lifting. But beware: DfE officials don't like groups to become too hugger-mugger with commercial companies for fear that they might try to circumvent the procurement rules.

Project-management companies are subject to the same rules. Successful proposer groups are now given a 'lead in' budget by the department and told to procure whatever professional services they require, but because public money is involved they're still bound by procurement law and any sort of quid pro quo along the lines discussed is strictly forbidden. It doesn't matter how much help your group has received from an experienced project-management company prior to approval, you cannot pay it to provide further help unless it submits the best bid in response to your Invitation to Tender.

Nevertheless, you'll still receive offers of help from project management companies who believe, rightly or wrongly, that the pro bono support they've given you will create a sense of moral obligation on your part to hire them post-approval. If you choose to exploit that, that's your choice. But my advice is to follow both the spirit and letter of the law.

The Evaluation Matrix

In 2012, the DfE published 'how to apply' guidance on its website setting out the criteria by which those applying to open schools in 2013 were to be judged – the 'evaluation matrix'. Given that this is the third version of this matrix, it's unlikely to change much from now on, but with the civil service you never know. One thing I've learnt since getting involved in free schools is that large bureaucracies are unstable, constantly evolving entities. Since 1995, the bit of the civil service responsible for education has changed its name five times: from the Department for Education to the Department for Education and Employment, then to the Department for Education and Skills, then to the Department for Children, Schools and Families and, finally, back to the Department for Education again. Whatever stationer has the concession for the department's headed notepaper and business cards must have made a fortune by now.

Provided your proposal isn't a total wash-out, it will be passed on to an approval panel, who will then award marks section by section to arrive at a total score. Assessing how much effort to lavish on each of the sections is tricky because the DfE won't disclose what percentage of the overall mark is allocated to each one. For 2012 openers, my advice was to pay particular attention to the educational plan, the 'evidence of demand' and the capacity and capability sections, but that wasn't based on any inside information. The weightings are kept secret partly because the DfE doesn't want groups to be able to game the system by focusing on one area and neglecting another. But it's also to make it harder for disappointed applicants to contest the decision. There's another reason, too. If the DfE doesn't make public exactly how the scoring works, it means nothing's fixed in stone. There's more wiggle room. The approval panels can exercise a little discretion and, more importantly, so can the ministers when it comes to making a final decision.

The one piece of inside dope I can offer is to pay a good deal of attention to the curriculum. For 2013 openers, this was worth a grand total of three points in the evaluation matrix, but that's set to change in future years and that's as it should be. The more deeply I've got into this field, the more I've realised how important a school's curriculum is. In particular, I've become an evangelist for a knowledge-based curriculum and in due course I hope to develop templates for both primaries and secondaries. If the idea of a knowledge-based curriculum appeals to you – if you think that a school's primary purpose is to transmit knowledge from one generation to the next – email me at newfreeschool@gmail.com and I'll send you what I have so far.

The Interview

If your approval is deemed sufficiently strong, you'll be summoned to appear before one of the approval panels. I've got a top tip for you here: make sure you turn up on the right day. After my group had submitted its first application, we received the call-up and I proudly ushered all the team members into the lobby of Sanctuary Buildings on Great Smith Street, the DfE's headquarters. 'We're here to see ——', I said, giving the name of the civil servant I'd been told to ask for. Five minutes later the official appeared with a bemused look on his face. Our appointment was for the following week.

It was excruciatingly embarrassing, not least because the point of these interviews is for an approval panel to assess just how competent your group is. Yes, they'll probe you about the weaker aspects of your proposal, but they'll also be forming a judgement about your overall reliability. What the panellists are trying to work out is: can they, in good conscience, recommend that the Secretary of State approves your application? Some members of the panel will be outside experts – retired heads, accountants – but some will be career civil servants. The last thing they want is to rubber-stamp a school that subsequently turns out to be a high-profile failure.

By all means mug up before your interview and make

sure your group can answer all the questions that the panel is likely to throw at you. But also think about making a good impression. Your aim should be to radiate calm authority. You want to assure the members that you're a safe pair of hands. You're not going to cock anything up.

Easier said than done, of course, and it helps if you turn up on the right day.

The Minister

Officially, the person who approves your proposal is the Secretary of State, but in reality he'll delegate this power to one of his ministers. In the case of the 2012 and 2013 applicants, that person was Lord Hill of Oareford, the Under-Secretary of State for Schools.

The way it works is that the Free Schools Directorate – the team of over 100 civil servants in the department responsible for delivering the free schools policy – will produce a list of applicants for the minister to consider. They'll be divided into two bands: Band A and Band B. If your application is in Band A, you're home and dry. These are the schools that the civil servants are recommending for ministerial approval. If you're in Band B, your fate is hanging in the balance. The minister will only be able to approve a certain number of schools because of budgetary constraints. So he has to choose which schools in Band B to approve in addition to the ones in Band A.

This is where political considerations come into play. Is the school in an area where there's acute basic need? Is it in the bottom half of the 'deprivation index'? Is it being set up by a faith group? Generally speaking, the present government doesn't have a problem with faith schools – and free schools set up by faith groups can reserve fifty per cent of their places for members of their particular faith. Nevertheless, if there are already several free schools being set up by faith groups in Band A, the minister won't want to pick too many more from Band B. Politically, he'll want to avoid giving the impression that the free-schools policy is being monopolized by religious zealots. (Of the 102 schools approved in the third wave, thirty-three characterised themselves as faith schools and, of those, twenty were proposing to select some pupils on the basis of faith.)

5

Approaching the Finish Line

Once your application has been approved, you enter the 'pre-opening stage'. With a few exceptions, this stage is supposed to last for about a year. Of the sixty-five free-school groups that were approved in September 2011, most were expected to open in September 2012. And the same timeline applied to the batch approved in July 2012. The DfE will expect the vast majority of free schools to open within approximately twelve months of being approved. In my view, that's optimistic. The issue isn't the amount of work you need to do in this period – though it's immense, obviously – but the need to hit a series of targets according to a rigid timetable. The task is complicated by the fact that you need to hit these targets in the correct sequence. Consequently, if you miss one deadline, you'll miss the rest. If you find yourself in that situation, you'll have to decide whether to stick to the plan or postpone the opening of your school by a year. My advice is to postpone.

The easiest way to explain this is to begin with the final target and work backwards. Your aim should be to open in September with a full complement of pupils. Remember, if you open with fewer pupils than planned you're going to have difficulty paying your bills. This is why the DfE pays so much attention to the 'evidence of demand' section in your application. It knows that the greatest threat to any school's survival, not just a free school's, is failure to fill its roll. When it approved the first wave of free schools it wasn't as vigilant about this as it should have been and, as a result, several of them were under-subscribed. (I don't mean there were spaces further up the school. I mean there were spaces in their opening year groups, whether Reception for primaries or Year 7 for secondaries.) In addition, some of the schools approved in the second wave – such as the Newham Free School – fell by the wayside when they failed to sign up enough pupils. The department won't want to find itself in that position again if it can help it.

Now, you might think that provided you can get your school open, being under-subscribed is the DfE's problem. If you don't manage to get a full complement of Reception or Year 7 pupils, the DfE is hardly going to allow your school to fail. So why worry?

Two reasons.

First, you can't depend upon the DfE to bail you out. Local authorities suffer financial penalties if the community schools they're responsible for fail to fill their rolls. Why should free schools be treated any differently? OK, Michael Gove probably won't want to make an example of any free schools in this way because the policy is his baby. But who's to say he'll still be Secretary of State by the time your school opens? He might have been replaced by a Lib Dem. Worse, the coalition might have collapsed. If the new Secretary of State in an incoming Labour government discovers that one of the last government's beloved free schools is under-subscribed you can bet your bottom dollar he won't hesitate to impose swingeing penalties.

Second, even if the Secretary of State bails you out in year one, you've still got future years to worry about. As any head teacher or chair of governors will tell you, being under-subscribed is like catching a cold that can quickly develop into pneumonia. As soon as local parents get wind of the fact that your school is struggling to fill its roll, they won't want to send their children there. If you open twenty-five pupils short of a full Reception or Year 7 cohort in year one, chances are you'll be fifty pupils short in year two. It won't take long before things spiral out of control.

Take the example of Christ the King, a new comprehensive in Liverpool that was opened with great fanfare by Ed Balls in 2009. Described as 'more than just a school', the £24 million new build embraced the very latest thinking about teaching and learning. Instead of classrooms, pupils would congregate in 'home base areas' and instead of teachers they'd be taught by 'progress leaders'. Knowsley Council hailed it as the beginning of 'the biggest transformation of education in the borough for two generations'.

Unfortunately, parents weren't quite as enthusiastic about this trendy new approach. The school was undersubscribed in its first year and, as a result, only managed to fill about half its places in 2010. The upshot was that in January 2011, by which time the local authority knew just how few parents had applied for places the following year, it was announced that Christ the King would close. It lasted exactly two years.

So you need to make sure your school is fully subscribed from the very first day. That should be your final and most important target and almost everything else you do in the twelve-month lead-up to that point should be geared to that.

One thing some free schools do to mitigate this risk is to admit more than one year group when they open for the first time – the Free School Norwich, for instance – but I wouldn't recommend this. It makes it harder to plan the teaching and learning at your school during the ramp-up phase and it's a sure-fire way to alienate the surrounding schools who will have to deal with the headache of pupils transferring from their schools to yours. Admitting pupils to your sixth form at the same time as you admit Year 7s can work, but anything more ambitious should be avoided.

Admissions

In their first year, free schools generally operate outside the admissions framework coordinated by local admissions authorities. That means they aren't obliged to offer places to applicants at the same time as other taxpayer-funded schools. If they want to, they can go out with offers later in the year, which is precisely what some of the 2011 openers did. Perfectly understandable, because they didn't want to make any offers until they were certain that there'd be a school for children to come to. But it was a mistake – and the fact that some free schools in the first wave were undersubscribed can be traced back to that mistake.

The difficulty they faced when they eventually did get all their ducks in a row was that the majority of the parents they were offering places to had already accepted places elsewhere. They'd made a decision and become acclimatized to it. They'd worked out the best way to get to those schools in the morning. In some cases, they'd even bought the uniform. Of course, some parents weren't necessarily happy about sending their sons or daughters to the schools they'd accepted places at, but they were inhibited by simple good manners from causing inconvenience by changing their minds. The simple truth is that, for all sorts of reasons, a parent who's already accepted a place at another school is less likely to accept your offer than one who hasn't.

The offer day for state secondary schools in England is 1 March and, from 2013, the offer day for primaries will be 16 April. That's when the local authority letter containing an offer will land on parents' doormats. If you're going to stand a chance of filling your Reception or Year 7 classes you need to make sure your offers land on parents' doormats at exactly the same time.

The Funding Agreement

The main reason some of the 2011 openers didn't make those deadlines is because they hadn't signed their Funding Agreements with the Secretary of State at that point. This is a doorstopper of a contract setting out the terms on which the Secretary of State has agreed to finance your school. If you think of the set-up process as an elaborate courtship with the Secretary of State, signing the Funding Agreement is when you plight your troth. There's no going back after this. It's the point of no return. Once he's signed your Funding Agreement, he won't be able to stop you opening the following September.

For free-school groups nervous about whether they're going to make their opening deadline or not, the signing of the Funding Agreement is hugely reassuring. Before that point, there's always a degree of anxiety – not least the uncertainty about whether the Secretary of State is going to give your school the final green light. Which is why some of the 2011 openers were reluctant to make any offers until they had the Secretary of State's signature on the dotted line.

Once again, it's all perfectly understandable. But the solution isn't to delay going out with offers until you've signed your Funding Agreement. It's to make damn sure you sign the Agreement in time to make offers on the relevant days, i.e. 1 March if you're a secondary, 16 April if you're a primary.

The Consultation

You'll need to tick a whole warehouse full of boxes before the Secretary of State will be willing to sign your Funding Agreement, but the most important of these is the statutory consultation. This is a requirement of the Academies Act 2010 thanks to an amendment slipped in at the last minute by a peer opposed to the policy. Section 10 of the Act stipulates that proposers of free schools must consult such people as they consider appropriate. You don't necessarily have to change anything about your school in response to their views; all you have to do is ask them what they think. It doesn't sound particularly onerous, but it's the very vagueness of the wording that makes it such a legal minefield. The Act imposes a legal obligation on proposer groups to carry out a consultation before establishing their free schools, but it doesn't say whom, exactly, they should consult.

By common consent, failure to carry out an adequate consultation is the ground on which free-schools groups are most likely to be legally challenged by opponents of the policy. That means it's not something you can afford to be lackadaisical about. You have to get it absolutely right. In short, you need a good lawyer.

The DfE won't provide any legal advice (see Chapter 3) and neither will the New Schools Network. If you choose to work with a project-management company, it will have a lawyer on its books, but don't assume he or she will get this right. You mustn't be afraid to question their advice and, if necessary, seek a second opinion. This is a complex and fluid area of public law that has yet to be tested in the courts so you need to be advised by a shrewd and experienced education lawyer. My group got lucky. The project-management company helping us, E. C. Harris, had a relationship with Graham Burns, one of the best education lawyers in the business. Try and get someone of his calibre to advise you. Better yet, get him. This is the most perilous stage of your journey – it's a tightrope stretched across a snake pit – and you cannot afford to put a foot wrong.

What follows is some general advice about your consultation that is in no way intended to be a substitute for proper legal counsel. Think of this as a rudimentary checklist to help you assess the lawyer who's already advising you. If he or she hasn't already flagged up these things, you need another lawyer.

Include as many people as possible

The Eden Primary School in Haringey, one of the 2011 openers, didn't consult all the parents in the area and, on that basis, the parents of a child at a neighbouring primary school argued that the consultation was invalid. The case was taken up by a left-wing lawyer and, for a while, it looked as if the parents would petition the courts to prevent the school from opening. The group's defence was that they'd sent a copy of their consultation letter to the headmaster of the school in question and asked him to make all the parents of children at the school aware of its proposal. In the end, that was sufficient to deter the parents from pursuing the case, but the lesson is clear. When it comes to deciding who to include and who to leave out, err on the side of liberality.

Include your admissions policy

Again, you'll be vulnerable to legal challenge if you don't. After all, how can the head teachers of the surrounding schools assess the likely impact of your school if they don't know what its admissions arrangements will be? Oh, and make sure your admissions policy is compatible with the School Admissions Code of Practice. If it isn't, you may have to start your consultation all over again.

Allow at least six weeks for responses

That may sound like a long time, but if your consultation is any shorter you'll be vulnerable to the charge that you haven't given people long enough to react.

Try and identify the location of your site

Again, if you aren't able to do this, you'll be vulnerable to challenge, in this case because the people you've consulted can't be expected to respond to the proposed new school if they don't know where it's going to be.

Allow the Secretary of State sufficient time to digest your findings

The Secretary of State cannot sign a Funding Agreement with you until your consultation has been completed and he's had time to review it because Section 9 of the Academies Act – another last-minute amendment – requires him to take into account the impact of establishing the free school on maintained schools, academies and further education institutions in the area. He can't do that if he hasn't had time to absorb your consultation.

The Timetable

At this point, it should be dawning on you that you're locked into a pretty rigid timetable. Suppose your free school is a secondary. That means you need to go out with offers on 1 March and that, in turn, means you need to sign your Funding Agreement by 28 February. If you're going to allow the Secretary of State a month to digest your consultation, that means completing it by 31 January and, if it takes a minimum of six weeks to carry out, that means starting it on 15 December at the very latest. (If your free school is a primary, you can push everything back by six weeks.)

The deal breaker for lots of free-school groups will be the fourth item on my list of things you need to do in your consultation: identify your site. What if you want to open a secondary, but don't have a site by 15 December? Should you abandon all hope and resign yourself to postponing by a year? That question is complicated by planning considerations. What if you've got your eye on a site but haven't yet applied for planning permission? Is there any point in naming it in your consultation?

My advice is to name the site you think you're most likely to end up in and hope for the best. After all, you need to have pinned down a building – and be very confident you're going to get planning permission – by the relevant offer day. If you haven't, going out with offers will simply be too risky. You really don't want to find yourself in the position of having a full complement of pupils by September but with nowhere to put them. That will be a blow to your school's credibility from which it will never recover. Either you do end up nailing down the building you've named in your consultation by the relevant offer day, in which case you go out with offers, or you don't, in which case you don't. And not naming the site in the consultation will expose you to the risk of challenge.

Marketing

If you're going to fill your roll, you need to open for applications as soon as possible after your school has been approved. You'll have already secured plenty of commitments from prospective parents in the course of compiling 'evidence of demand'. Now you need to start converting these to concrete applications. The rule of thumb is that you need at least three times as many applicants as there are places if you're going to avoid being under-subscribed.

Don't ask me why, but the rule holds fast for every type of school. That means an aggressive marketing campaign.

It's helpful at this point to think of the neighbouring schools catering to the same age group as competitors. They'll certainly think of you that way. And they have a huge head start in that they're already up and running, in some cases for hundreds of years. They will hold 'open days' – often as early as September – for prospective parents to visit their schools. They will press-gang their most winsome pupils into showing parents round and these 'ambassadors' will be under strict instructions to avoid the fourteen-year-olds smoking behind the bike shed and instead make a bee-line for the state-of-the-art IT suite. The parents will emerge from these sessions in a state of mild euphoria, convinced the school in question is a cross between Hogwarts and Grange Hill.

How can you possibly compete? Well, you have one ace up your sleeve, which is that parents will be risking nothing by applying to your school provided you're operating outside the normal admissions framework for the first year. That means parents won't have to name your school as one of their preferences on the standard application form. Consequently, they won't be jeopardizing their chances of getting into any of the neighbouring schools if they apply to yours. Their application will be considered *alongside* the application they've made as part of the formal application process, not *instead of* it. If they meet your over-subscription criteria they'll be offered a place at your school *in addition to* the offer they receive from their local authority. They've nothing to lose and everything to gain.

Of course, this will only reassure parents up to a point. They'll also want to know how seriously they can take an offer from your school if they're lucky enough to get one. What guarantee do they have that your school will actually open? They won't want to risk turning down an offer from any of the neighbouring schools if there's a chance there won't be anywhere for their children to go in September.

When I was asked that question, I was able to reply that if we hadn't nailed down our site and signed a Funding Agreement by 1 March we simply wouldn't make any offers. Night after night I stood up in front of groups of parents – whether in town halls, primary schools or in meetings convened above pubs – and told them that if they received an offer from the West London Free School that meant the school would be open in September. And so it proved to be.

The Head Teacher

To a great extent, how successful you are in persuading parents to apply to your school and, in due course, accept your offers will depend on how credible they think you are. One particular question I was asked repeatedly was along the lines of: 'If my son's appendix burst, I wouldn't take him to a hospital run by patients. Why should I send him to a school run by parents?' It helps at this point if you can introduce them to your head teacher, the person who'll actually be running the school.

You need to recruit your head as soon as possible. It doesn't matter if he or she can't resign from their current post immediately. The key thing is to get them on board so they can start meeting parents. Your project lead at the DfE and the helpful people at the New Schools

Network can advise about how best to find a head – and you can use some of your 'lead in' budget to pay for an ad in *The Times Educational Supplement* (or hire a recruitment firm). Make sure your ad is well written. I've been a professional writer for over twenty-five years, but I don't think I've ever taken as much trouble over anything as our head-teacher ad. It must have gone through a dozen drafts. Here's what it said:

> Most people say it can't be done. An all-ability secondary school that asks every child to learn Latin and do at least eight academic GCSEs or IGCSEs? Impossible. That expects every pupil to go on to a good university? Absurd. That takes children from the very poorest backgrounds and gives them the confidence and ambition to take on the world? Stop dreaming.
>
> Over 1,000 local parents and teachers in West London think it can be done. We believe that any child, no matter what their ability, can access an academically demanding curriculum provided they're taught in the right way. This requires a thorough knowledge of best practice, a familiarity with the latest academic research and a willingness to innovate and experiment. It requires a core of outstanding teachers, devoted to constantly improving their own and their pupils' performance. Above all, it requires you – a visionary leader willing to take on the challenge of a lifetime.
>
> You will:
>
> - Assemble your own team and design a school from the ground up.
> - Introduce a new generation of children to the best that has been thought and said.

- Develop a radical pedagogy capable of delivering a core body of knowledge to a diverse group of children.
- Be the public face of the most talked-about educational project in the country.

We believe it is only by reaching for the impossible that you discover what's possible. Our motto is '*Sapere aude*' – dare to learn – and that will apply to the staff as well as the pupils. Do you have the strength of character and the intellectual ability to lead this project? If so, we'd like you to apply to become the head of the West London Free School.

Mr Packer

We had over 120 applications and John McIntosh and I spent an exhausting afternoon at his flat in Fulham whittling them down to a shortlist of eight. John and I then sat in a room at E. C. Harris, alongside Alice Hudson, the headmistress of an outstanding faith school in Acton, and most of the members of my steering group, and interviewed them.

'You'll know who the right person is as soon as they step foot in the room,' said John and he was right. All eight candidates were strong, but Thomas Packer stood out. Not only was he more than qualified for the job, having already served as a headmaster of two successful schools, but he had the X-Factor. With his three-piece suit and fob watch, he looked like a headmaster from central casting. He exuded authority from every pore. Just looking at him, I knew his presence as the headmaster of the West London Free School would be all the assurance that most parents would need. With him at the helm, we'd have no problem filling our places.

The Risk Register

There are plenty of other things you'll need to do before you're ready to open, including recruiting a deputy head and the rest of the staff, but the DfE and the New Schools Network should be able to help you with all of those. The reason I've focused on making sure your school is fully subscribed is because I regard that as at the top of the risk register. Think of that as your number-one priority and work backwards from there.

You may think I'm being overcautious, particularly if you're doubtful you can hit all these targets. Maybe you'll decide to risk making offers on the relevant offer day even if you haven't secured a site and signed a Funding Agreement. Or maybe you'll decide to wait until you have ticked those boxes and only then go out with offers, even though that means there's a risk of not filling all your places. All I can tell you is that my group wasn't prepared to take those risks. Thanks to the prudent advice of our lawyer and our project manager, we were able to nail down a site, complete our consultation and sign a Funding Agreement by 28 February and go out with offers on 1 March. As a result, we were fully subscribed when we opened on 7 September 2011.

6

Future Proofing

OK, you opened on time and you're fully subscribed. Well done. Take a bow. But what if there's a change of government? Ed Balls has knifed Ed Miliband in the run-up to the election, he's now the Prime Minister and one of his first acts is to ennoble Fiona Millar and make her the Secretary of State for Education. What can you do to protect your school from Baroness Millar?

On the face of it, you don't need to worry because Clause 82 of your Funding Agreement says the Secretary of State needs to give you seven years' notice if he or she wants to terminate. Not only will that enable you to continue educating all the children at your school up to the end of the sixth form, it means that a hostile Labour government would have to last two terms to see the termination through.

However, there are other clauses in the Funding Agreement that a Secretary of State determined to shut down your school could invoke. Clause 91C, for instance, grants him or her the power to terminate immediately if they decide that a member of your governing body is 'not a suitable person'. I don't think it would take Fiona Millar long to conclude I wasn't a suitable person to be the governor of a taxpayer-funded school – she's said as much already. Then there's Clause 12A, which states that one of the conditions of your grant continuing to be paid is that 'the school will be at the heart of its community, promoting community cohesion'. That, too, could be exploited by a hostile Secretary of State.

Realistically, though, it isn't very likely that a Labour Secretary of State, however unsympathetic, would try to shut down free schools – and Stephen Twigg, the current shadow education secretary, has said he'll leave the successful ones well alone. It would look petty and vindictive and they would be vulnerable to the charge of punishing children for the sins of the previous administration. More probable is that they would insist your school behaved more like a bog-standard comprehensive as a condition of continuing to receive government funding. So you'd have to teach the national curriculum, transfer responsibility for your admissions to the local authority and sign up to the national pay and conditions arrangements agreed between the government and the teaching unions. In other words, you'd cease to be a free school in all but name.

I raised these concerns about the Funding Agreement with various officials at the DfE before signing it. Couldn't it be made Baroness Millar-proof? I argued that our school wouldn't be 'free' in any meaningful sense if its much-vaunted independence was contingent on the good-will of the Secretary of State. How could I urge parents to send their children to the West London Free School if there was no guarantee that its distinctive ethos and curriculum would survive a change of government? What was the point of creating this new tier of schools if their freedoms weren't protected in the Funding Agreement?

The officials were unimpressed. They said it would be 'unconstitutional' to fetter the Secretary of State's successors by making free schools inviolable. In any case, there wouldn't be any point in protecting their autonomy in their Funding Agreements since a hostile government could simply enact primary legislation to override those documents.

After pushing back for a bit and trying in vain to enlist the support of Michael Gove, I decided my group had no choice but to sign the Funding Agreement as written. Nevertheless, that doesn't mean we should resign ourselves to allowing an unsympathetic Secretary of State to ride roughshod over us should there be a change of government. On the contrary, I think there are several ways to protect a free school's autonomy:

Be popular

If your school is over-subscribed it's going to be harder for Baroness Millar to intervene than if it's under-subscribed. Not only will she lack a *casus belli*, she'll risk alienating all those Labour voters in the surrounding area who either have children at your school or hope to in a few years' time. If your school is in a Labour marginal – as the West London Free School is – the sitting MP won't thank her for that.

Be successful

Again, if your school is getting above-average examination results, a hostile Secretary of State will lack an excuse to interfere. It would look as though he or she preferred mediocrity for all to excellence for some. Remember, British education is not exactly in rude good health. In the past ten years or so, the standing of our schoolchildren in the international league tables has plummeted while countries like China, Hong Kong, Singapore, South Korea and Taiwan have surged ahead. In that context, it would be difficult for a Secretary of State for Education to penalize a school that was getting excellent results.

Make sure you have an above-average number of pupils on free school meals

You'll be more vulnerable to attack if all the pupils at your school come from well-off backgrounds. That will enable Baroness Millar to brand your school 'elitist' and accuse you of 'gerrymandering' the admissions process to select only middle-class children. (Remember the 'bankers' school'?) Consequently, you should do what you can to make sure the percentage of children on free school meals at your school is above the national average (currently just under one in five). From 2013, you'll be allowed to reserve a set number of places for children receiving free school meals and I urge you to consider that if you think you aren't going to get very many otherwise.

Try not to jeopardize the survival of any neighbouring schools

If your school is ticking all three of the above boxes, the only remaining excuse a Labour Secretary of State will have to interfere is if it's having a negative impact on a school near by. At one point, Stephen Twigg said he'd apply that 'test' to free schools. In practice, what this means is he'll try to claim that the reason a neighbouring school is under-subscribed (which is unlikely, given the current population boom) is because there was never sufficient basic need to justify setting up a free school in the area. Now, the sensible thing to do in those circumstances would be to shut down the failing school, not the free school, but when it comes to politicians you cannot rely on their being sensible. Consequently, when drawing up your admissions arrangements you need to think about the potential impact your school will have on any struggling schools in the neighbourhood. That doesn't necessarily mean you have to make sure your catchment areas don't overlap – after all, the point of the free-schools policy is to increase parental choice. But try to make sure you're not sourcing *all* your pupils from exactly the same area as a nearby failing school. In the case of the West London Free School, we admit half the children according to distance from the school gates and half via a lottery within a three-mile radius. In that way, we've diluted any negative impact our school is likely to have on any of the neighbouring schools.

Purchase a site

In the long term, your best defence against a hostile Secretary of State is to own your site. Now, in all likelihood, the DfE will transfer the freehold of the site your school is in to the charitable trust you've set up to run the school – either that, or the trust will have a 125-year peppercorn lease. However, Clause 101 of the Funding Agreement states that in the event of termination all the assets of that trust will be transferred to the Secretary of State. This is known as 'the reversion clause'. Consequently, you'll be in a much stronger bargaining position if you're able to raise the money to purchase a site before signing the Funding Agreement. Once you've done that, you can place that site under the control of a separate trust and then have that trust lease the site to the school. That way, if the Secretary of State terminates, he or she won't get your site. That will be a big disincentive if they're thinking of shutting down your school because they won't have anywhere to put all the pupils. Of course, most groups won't have the resources to purchase a site, but as soon as your school is established you can set about raising money to buy additional facilities – playing fields, swimming pool, sixth-form building, etc. Provided these are owned by a separate trust, the Secretary of State won't be able to get hold of them in the event of termination. The school he or she will end up with will be pretty threadbare compared to the free school they've just shut down and, knowing that, the Secretary of State will be reluctant to close your school.

A Work in Progress

The government's free-schools policy is constantly evolving and if this guide is to remain useful it will need to be updated again. For that reason, I'd welcome any feedback from proposer groups currently trying to navigate the set-up process. Tell me which parts of this book you've found helpful and which parts you now consider out of date. If you think I'm being overcautious about some of the risks, such as not filling all your places, let me know. Over the past two years, I've got to know quite a few of the proposer groups out there and I've tried to draw on their experience as well as my own for this book. But the more feedback I am given, the better future editions will be. Please contact me at newfreeschool@gmail.com.

So, goodbye and good luck. I hope I haven't put you off. If you're ever feeling blue, come and visit Mr Packer and me at the West London Free School. At the very least, it should prove that it's possible to achieve your dream. And I promise not to do a Jonathan Fingerhut.

Afterword

At the beginning of 2010 I was starting to lose heart because my group still hadn't found a site. We'd contacted all the local estate agents, searched on the Register of Surplus Public Sector Assets – we'd even looked on Google Earth. Nothing. Then I heard about this free-school group in Camden who'd carried out a *Fugitive*-style sweep of the local area. They'd literally searched 'every gas station, residence, warehouse, farmhouse, henhouse, outhouse and dog house' in Camden Town and – bingo – they'd found a site. I decided to do likewise.

We divided our neighbourhood into twelve different 'quadrants' and each member of the steering group spent an afternoon cycling around his or her section and taking photographs of potential sites. We then sat down round my kitchen table to see if any were worth pursuing.

The most suitable site in my 'quadrant' was the King Fahad Academy, a private Muslim all-through school owned by the Kingdom of Saudi Arabia. It seemed to be operating well below full capacity and we approached the headmistress to see if she might be willing to rent us the unused classrooms. She informed us that, contrary to appearances, all the classrooms were in constant use.

More promising was an empty secondary school tucked away behind some large iron gates on Little Ealing Lane that another member of my group stumbled across. This turned out to be the King Fahad Academy for Girls, which had closed in 2007. As far as we could tell, the only use being made of it was as a madrasa at the weekend.

We managed to contact the relevant officials at the Saudi embassy and were told that the Kingdom didn't want to sell the school but might be willing to lease it to us. They arranged for us to go and look round to see if we wanted to make an offer.

It was perfect. Not only was the site large enough for a 4-Form Entry secondary school – 840 pupils at full capacity – it had an incredible array of facilities: assembly hall, sports hall, science labs ... you name it. It even had a huge playground. We came away convinced we'd found our school. The gods were smiling on us at last.

We then embarked on a frantic period of activity in which we tried to draft a lease offer we thought would be both acceptable to the Kingdom and within our budget. At this stage, the steering group really came into its own. The architects drew up some plans, the chartered surveyor assessed their feasibility and the quantity surveyor costed them, all free of charge. It was the Big Society in action.

We proposed that we lease the buildings for a twenty-five-year period at an annual rent of roughly half a million pounds, but that payment would begin only after the cost of refurbishing the buildings had been recovered in the form of unpaid rent. We estimated that the cost of bringing the school up to code when it came to fire regulations, disabled access, etc., was about £4 million, so we were proposing to pay no rent for the first eight years. It sounds optimistic, but according to the embassy officials we'd been liaising with this offer would fly.

I submitted the proposal in writing to His Royal Highness Prince Mohammed bin Nawaf, the Saudi ambassador to the United Kingdom and Republic of Ireland, on 27 April 2010 and was expecting to hear back within a matter of days. We knew that the details of the lease agreement would have to be ironed out, so the sooner negotiations got started, the better. In addition, our quantity surveyor thought it would take about a year to carry out the necessary works. Consequently, if we wanted to open the West London Free School in 2011 as planned, we needed to get cracking.

After two weeks had elapsed and I still hadn't heard anything I began to worry. Phone calls to the embassy led to assurances that the offer had been received by Prince Mohammed and passed on to the Ministry of Foreign Affairs in Riyadh. His Royal Highness was just waiting for a formal response.

A month passed, followed by another and then another. At one point I was told that the school was actually owned by a member of the Saudi royal family and that he would be visiting London soon, whereupon a decision would be made. But his visit came and went and still I heard nothing.

One of the members of our group was in the Foreign Office and, after six months had passed, I asked him if he could find out what was causing the delay. He contacted a colleague in Riyadh who was able to track down the relevant official in the Saudi Foreign Ministry. He asked him why we hadn't had a reply.

'Ah yes, I know the letter you speak of,' he said. 'It has been passed on to me. The reason I haven't drafted a reply is that the Kingdom has never leased a government-owned building on foreign soil before and we have no way of assessing the offer. Is it a good offer? I have no idea.' He paused as the Foreign Office mandarin took this in.

'You know how it is, my friend. When someone proposes to do something that we officials have never done before we don't know how to react. When this letter crossed my desk I placed it at the bottom of my in-tray and now, whenever it floats to the top, I just send it back to the bottom again. No process, no response.'

To this day, I still haven't had an acknowledgement from the Saudi ambassador, let alone a reply. No process, no response.

In the course of setting up your free school you'll be tempted to come up with all sorts of creative solutions to the problems you encounter, particularly when it comes to finding a suitable site. Be warned: bureaucrats aren't keen on trying something that's never been done before. I've lost count of the number of conversations I've had with free-school proposers in which they've vented their frustration about the inflexibility of the officials they're having to deal with. They're particularly enraged when they've come up with a scheme that could save the taxpayer millions of pounds. To them, this sums up the shortcomings of career civil servants.

My advice is not to let this get to you. The fault doesn't lie in the personality of the bureaucrat, but in the nature of bureaucracy. Officials are obliged to operate within the rules and if they stray into a grey area they will always err on the side of caution precisely because they're dealing with taxpayers' money. It doesn't matter how good your idea is, if the officials cannot take it forward without drafting a new set of guidelines, you won't get very far. There's a process in place for coming up with new rules and, like everything else, it's complex, slow and subject to the vicissitudes of political fortune. No civil servant, however bold, is going to rewrite the rules to allow your group to do something that's never been done before.

So don't try to reinvent the wheel. That was a lesson my group was taught over and over again. There's room for innovation and experimentation, but it is in the ethos and curriculum of your school, not the manner in which you set it up. Like everyone trying to do something new, you have to learn not to try and do too many new things at once.

Acknowledgements

One of the nicest things about setting up a free school is the number of people willing to help. Indeed, the West London Free School now receives so many emails from people offering to give up their time for free we've had to employ someone to manage the volunteers.

Some people stand out. In particular, I'm thinking of the members of my steering group, most of whom were complete strangers to me before we embarked on this project: Jo Alexander, Charlie Ben-Nathan, Stefan Bojanowski, Kathryn Cooper, Chris Wieszczycki, Caroline Ffiske, Suzie Hobart, Ed Hobart, Simon Hugill, Cosmo Lush, John McIntosh, Justin Tooth, Tim Waters, Mustafa Erdem and my wife Caroline Bondy. (She wasn't a complete stranger, obviously.) Sitting round my dining-room table with this group of people, week after week, trying to figure out how to do this, was one of the best experiences of my life. This book is written in the first person, but the advice it contains is the distillation of our collective wisdom.

There are some others who deserve a special mention. First, there are the various officials in the Department for Education, particularly Fran Sims, who guided my group through the free schools set-up process and have patiently answered my follow-up questions about how the process has changed since. Then there's Rachel Wolf, the director of the New Schools Network. At various points in the writing of this book she has helped me clarify my thoughts. Particular thanks are also due to Louise Allanach, our project manager, Tom Legge, who can give Louise a run for her money as the best project manager in the business, Graham Burns, our lawyer, and Lara Newman, our chief nursemaid at the Education Funding Agency. Without their wise counsel my group would never have got through the process and they, too, have been good enough to answer the questions I've had in connection with this book.

Finally, a special mention should go to Thomas Packer, the headmaster of the West London Free School, and the team of teachers he's assembled. Entrusting your school to anyone is a leap of faith, but in this case they had to take a much bigger one. I hope this book helps you set up your free school, but at some point you will have to hand over the reins to the teachers. So far, our faith in Tom and his team has been repaid a thousand times over and I wish you the same luck we had in finding them. Never forget – it's all about the staff.